# Actual Factuals

CHOICE BOOKS OF KANSAS
7217 W MILLS AVE.
HUTCHINSON, KS 67505-9100
WE WELCOME YOUR RESPONSE

# ACTUAL FACTUALS

*with verses from the Bible*

## NANCY S. HILL

Tyndale House Publishers, Inc.
WHEATON, ILLINOIS

Visit Tyndale's exciting Web site at www.tyndale.com

© 1997 by Nancy S. Hill. All rights reserved.
Cover photos copyright © 1997 by Dan Stultz. All rights reserved.

Unless otherwise stated, Scripture quotations are taken from *The Living Bible,* copyright ©
1971 owned by assignment by KNT Charitable Trust. All rights reserved.

Scripture quotations marked NIV are taken from the *Holy Bible,* New International Version®.
NIV® Copyright © 1973, 1978, 1984 by International Bible Society. Used by permission of
Zondervan Publishing House. All rights reserved.

Scripture quotations marked RSV are taken from the *Holy Bible,* Revised Standard Version,
copyright © 1946, 1952, 1971 by the Division of Christian Education of the National Council
of the Churches of Christ in the United States of America, and are used by permission. All
rights reserved.

Scripture quotations marked KJV are taken from the *Holy Bible,* King James Version.

Scripture quotations marked TEV are taken from *The Bible in Today's English Version.* Old
Testament copyright: © American Bible Society, 1976; New Testament copyright: © American
Bible Society, 1966, 1971, 1976.

**Library of Congress Cataloging-in-Publication Data**

Hill, Nancy S., date
  Actual factuals / Nancy S. Hill.
     p.   cm.
  Includes bibliographical references and index.
  ISBN 0-8423-0035-X (pbk.)
  1. Meditations.   I. Title.
BV4832.2.H536   1997
242—dc20                                                                    96-46019

Printed in the United States of America

03  02  01  00  99  98  97
 7   6   5   4   3   2   1

To my parents,
Ret. Cmdr. Edward S. and Mary Siergiej,
for always telling me I should, could, and would;
and to my husband, Zack,
the love of my life,
who showed me the way

# CONTENTS ━━━━━━━━━━

# How did those sneakers get such a strange name?

It's a name almost everyone is familiar with, but few know of its origin. The product is sneakers, and the brand name is Adidas. In 1920 a German man named Adolph Dassler created the company that produces the popular athletic shoes. Known by his friends as Adi, Adolph added his nickname to his last name and formed Adidas.

We might think that a certain brand of shoes can improve our running or protect our feet. In a practical sense, that may be true. A better way to bolster our feet, in a spiritual sense, is to ask God's blessing for guidance of their activity. The Bible says, "The steps of good men are directed by the Lord. He delights in each step they take. If they fall it isn't fatal, for the Lord holds them with his hand" (Psalm 37:23-24). Others will be able to recognize God as our "brand name" if our feet follow his will.

# 2

# When can age be deceiving?

Some say that age is just a number; but for two unsuspecting individuals, it presented some unusual problems in their lives. A 1979 election caught Alice Blattler off guard when she was denied the opportunity to vote. According to town records, she was deceased. Alice explained that she was very much alive but received no response. Frustrated, Alice decided that since she was dead, there was no need to pay taxes. It wasn't long after her tax money stopped arriving that officials changed their records and listed Alice as living.

Englishman Matt Brooks, 63, was tired of working at his job as a furnaceman. While applying for early retirement, Matt discovered that he had made a big mistake during his life. Records revealed that he was not 63 but 79 years old. Matt's application for "early retirement" was 14 years late.

Both Alice and Matt discovered that the years that make up our age can go quickly and sometimes without our awareness. Most of us tend to think that we'll always have more time—that we can put things off and someday have the luxury of planning for our future. The Bible says that we should ask, "Lord, help me to realize how brief my time on earth will be. Help me to know that I am here for but a moment more" (Psalm 39:4). If we think of every day as potentially our last, we will be much more likely to pay attention to and treasure the people and things that matter most.

# 3

## When is your gas tank most dangerous?

It would seem that a full gas tank in a car would be more dangerous and likely to explode than an empty tank. In reality, an empty gas tank can cause the most problems for someone trying to work on a car. Gasoline only burns if it is mixed with air. The less full the tank is, the more room there is for air and highly flammable vapor. When mechanics have to drain the tank in order to do work that might produce sparks, they fill it with water first. Water pushes the air and vapor out of the tank and lessens the danger of an explosion.

Explosions and fire capture our attention. That's why God used an unusual fire when he wanted to speak to Moses, who was busy tending his sheep. The Bible describes this event for us, saying, "There the angel of the Lord appeared to him in flames of fire from within a bush. Moses saw that though the bush was on fire it did not burn up. So Moses thought, 'I will go over and see this strange sight—why the bush does not burn up.' When the Lord saw that he had gone over to look, God called to him from within the bush, 'Moses! Moses!'" (Exodus 3:2-4, NIV).

It is unlikely that we will ever see a burning bush, but God wants our attention just as much. We can use the story of Moses and the burning bush to remind ourselves that our relationship with God is very important. God knows we can be distracted easily and that it's often our soul that gets neglected as we go through our daily living. But if we saw something on fire, our reflexes would tell us to drop everything immediately and do something about the fire. We should protect and nurture our relationship with God by applying the same energy and urgency that we would use to fight a fire.

---

### 4

# Why didn't Americans want to change their currency?

In theory it was supposed to be less expensive for the taxpayer because it would last longer than the paper dollar. The problem was that it was so close to the size of a quarter, people kept trying to pay a dollar for a quarter's worth of merchandise. The offending coin was the Susan B. Anthony dollar. In addition, 20 or 50 of these coins were bulkier and heavier to carry than a 20- or 50-dollar bill. The public ultimately rejected the Anthony dollar and production was eventually stopped, but not without leaving the United States Department of the Treasury with 500 million unused coins. Other past attempts to change currency have also drawn disapproval: The Kennedy half-dollar, the Eisenhower dollar, and the two-dollar bill have been equally ignored. Americans simply didn't want to make the change.

Change is often hard. If the results aren't rewarding enough, there's really no motivation to try something different. The alternative coins and bills didn't offer a better way; in fact, they created extra problems. But there's one change that is definitely worth it. The Bible tells us that our lives will change for the better when we become God's children. It says, "Don't copy the behavior and customs of this world, but be a new and different person with a fresh newness in all you do and think. Then you will learn from your own experience how his ways will really satisfy you" (Romans 12:2). Experience a good change for a change.

## 5

# Why were people with a headache advised to chew a tree?

"Chew the bark of a willow tree" was the doctor's prescription used for thousands of years to ease pain. It wasn't until the 1800s that scientists understood why the willow bark, combined with the meadowsweet plant, relieved pain and reduced fever. Willow bark contains salicylic acid. A chemist named Karl Gerhardt tried to improve the acid by mixing it with another chemical because the acid irritated the stomach and mouth. The procedure was hard and time consuming, so eventually he abandoned the idea even though his results were good.

In 1897 a German chemist, who was trying to help his arthritic father, took another look at Gerhardt's experiments, and the concept of acetylsalicylic acid compound was reborn. Felix Hoffman and his partner Heinrich Dreser worked for the Bayer drug firm, which decided to manufacture the compound in powdered form. Synthetic willow bark was given a new name: "aspirin"—the *a* for *acetyl*, the *spir* for *spiraea* (the type of plant from which it came), and the *in* because this was a popular ending for medicine names. The pill form of aspirin reached the market in 1915.

We're always happy to get relief from our pain, and doctors and scientists are finding better ways to help us all the time. But no matter how many test tubes a scientist examines, he won't find a cure for hurt feelings. How can we fix our pain when we're disappointed, disillusioned, or discouraged? It may be possible to numb ourselves, but that's only a temporary solution. To find a cure, we need to call on Jesus Christ, the Great Physician. The Bible tells us, "He heals the brokenhearted and binds up their wounds" (Psalm 147:3, NIV). Couldn't we all use a little of his tender loving care?

# 6

## When can you buy an antique by scratching your nose?

We've seen comedy scenes where an unsuspecting observer goes to an auction and finds out he has bought something expensive simply by making normal movements that the auctioneer interpreted as bids. Does this happen at real-life auctions? Partially. People do go to auctions and make bids on objects by using signals. Body movements are used so that the bidding doesn't turn into a shouting match. The auctioneer finds it much less confusing to look for signals than to listen to voices. Also, bidders like to make movements so that other people at the sale don't really know who is bidding.

The most common signals of bidding are touching the nose or earlobe, wiggling the nose, lifting a hat, winking, or nodding. Do you have to sit totally still while visiting an auction? It's not necessary. People who are going to bid in the auction talk privately with the auctioneer beforehand and tell him which signal they will use. The movements from those people are the ones recognized by the auctioneer.

How should we "signal" to people to let them know what we want? Are we being demanding, harsh, or abrupt in order to reach our goals in a hurry? There is a better way. The Bible advises, "Gentle words cause life and health;

griping brings discouragement" (Proverbs 15:4). Take the time to be kind and to respect the feelings of others. When people receive pleasant signals from us, they will be encouraged. In the long run, we will go farther by creating a healthy environment for progress.

---

# 7

# When can a backlog be helpful?

You'd like to leave the office early, but there's a backlog of paperwork you have to finish first. It will take a concentrated effort to clear the pile of papers that have accumulated on your desk. You're even too busy to realize that the word *backlog* comes from the days when the only way to heat a house was to keep a fire burning constantly in the fireplace.

Making sure the fire lasted all night while people slept was a problem. Before going to bed, someone would put an enormous log, maybe as large as two feet thick, at the back of the fireplace. Smaller logs would be placed in front. Eventually the big log would heat up from the flames of the smaller kindling. Instead of bursting into flames itself, it would slowly smoulder all night long, emitting heat. In the morning the backlog would have left enough embers to relight the fire. That's why it refers to something that's left over or not all used up.

Sometimes we carry around a backlog of guilt for something that happened in the past. We feel as if it will never leave and that we'll be stuck with it forever. God doesn't want us to bear that burden. The Bible says, "Who will be my shield? I would have died unless the Lord had helped me. I screamed, 'I'm slipping, Lord!' and he was kind and saved me. Lord, when doubts fill my mind, when my heart is in turmoil, quiet me and give me renewed hope and cheer" (Psalm 94:16-19). When you become God's child, you are entitled to his protection against hurt, guilt, and fear. Don't let suffering smoulder. Call out to God, and he will warm you with his comfort.

# 8
# When do you let the "cat out of the bag"?

When you've unintentionally talked about something you were supposed to keep quiet, you might have found yourself apologizing for "letting the cat out of the bag." But what cat? What bag? The familiar feline phrase retells a little piece of American history.

Long ago at county fairs many merchants would sell small pigs. After a sale, the merchants would tie up the animal and place it in a bag. Once home, the customers would open the bag and release their purchase. Sometimes, to their surprise and dismay, they found that the merchant had been dishonest. Out of the bag would come the merchant's secret, which had been hidden all the way home. He had not put a pig into the bag, but—you guessed it—an ordinary cat.

When people keep things hidden, whether an object or something about themselves, it almost always causes problems. If we're not really all that we "advertise" ourselves to be, it is difficult to keep up the pretense since it takes more energy and is far more exhausting to act calm when we're anxious or cheerful when we're sad. It is possible, however, to make some changes so that we can become a genuine article—just start at the root of the trouble.

The Bible says, "So get rid of your feelings of hatred. Don't just pretend to be good! Be done with dishonesty and jealousy and talking about others behind their backs" (1 Peter 2:1). Don't keep Jesus Christ a secret. He has the power to release all of the bad tricks in our bags and set us free.

---

## 9

# How did a bathtub help solve a mystery?

Archimedes, an early Greek scientist, was given a mystery to solve by the king. Concerned about his crown, the king feared that the man who made his headpiece had replaced some of the gold with another metal and kept the real gold for himself. Archimedes was supposed to prove whether this accusation was true or false without destroying the crown.

The scientist-turned-sleuth thought hard about a solution for this problem, but nothing occurred to him until he was taking a bath one evening. As he lowered his body into the tub, the water rose up around him. Suddenly Archimedes had his answer!

He realized that everything of equal weight would displace or move an equal weight of water. Archimedes put the correct amount of gold that the crown was supposed to have into some water, measuring how much the water weighed that was displaced. Then he lowered the crown into the same amount of water and weighed that displaced water. He soon discovered that heavier metals other than gold must have been added to the crown because the crown's displaced water weighed more than the pure gold's displaced water did.

The king was worried that his crown was not as valuable as it was supposed to be. Whether we realize it or not, we have access to a crown for ourselves. Its value doesn't rely on something as superficial as gold. How can we get this crown?

The Bible tells us, "Happy is the man who doesn't give in and do wrong when he is tempted, for afterwards he will get as his reward the crown of life that God has promised those who love him" (James 1:12). This crown entitles us to an eternal place in heaven. No one can steal it or replace it with something less. The longer we have it, the more its value will appreciate. Don't get shortchanged by settling for anything less.

# How did cowboys carry their meals?

People are putting a lot more effort into food preparation these days. This hasn't always been the case. As America headed west in the early 1800s, cowboys had a fairly simple way of securing a meal. They cut meat into strips and dried it in the sun. The strips were put in saddlebags and were then pulled out when the cowboy was hungry.

Argentine cowboys, called gauchos, made their meals a little differently. They placed raw meat strips underneath their saddles. By the end of the day, the strips were cooked by the heat and tenderized by the rocking of the saddle. These meat strips had a Spanish name—*charqui,* meaning "dried meat." It might surprise you to know that we still eat this food. The beef "charqui" of yesterday has become our own "beef jerky."

Meat is better when it's tender instead of tough. People are, too. The Bible says, "Stop being mean, bad-tempered, and angry. Quarreling, harsh words, and dislike of others should have no place in your lives. Instead, be kind to each other, tenderhearted, forgiving one another, just as God has forgiven you because you belong to Christ" (Ephesians 4:31-32). We can ask Jesus to soften our hearts and make us sensitive to others. It will prepare us to do his will wherever we may go.

# Why are men's and women's bikes different?

Have you ever stopped to wonder why men's and women's bikes have crossbars in different places? The ideal shape for a bicycle frame is a triangle or diamond. Those shapes make the bike strong and able to support weight better. Men's bicycles, with the crossbar parallel to the ground, were built for top efficiency. The slanted crossbar on women's bikes, in contrast, was modified for a historical reason.

In the early 1890s the bar was "lowered" so that women wearing skirts could mount and pedal more easily. This bike was called the "safety bike," and its design has never been changed, even though the "skirt problem" ended long ago. Serious bikers, both male and female, use the male-frame bike when they are concerned about performance and durability.

Creating a way for women to ride bikes comfortably probably caused a stir in its day. If that little invention was impressive, consider the works of the Master Inventor. The Bible describes some of them: "In his hand are the depths of the earth, and the mountain peaks belong to him. The sea is his, for he made it, and his hands formed the dry land" (Psalm 95:4-5, NIV). Anything and everything man can create pales in comparison to what God has done. Thinking about his awesome powers reminds us of how mighty he was, is, and always will be.

# Why do birds fly in a V formation?

We don't often think of birds as having the ability to organize themselves. Yet they often fly in formation. How and why do they end up in a V shape? It has to do with air currents. The lead bird becomes the point of the V, slicing through the air and creating a current of V-shaped wind behind it. The other birds are helped along because whirlpools of wind form within the V shape and give an extra push forward. Scientists also think that birds see better while flying that way since their eyes are on the sides of their heads. The V gives birds the best view of the rest of their flock.

When birds have somewhere to go, they put all their energies into the journey. God has equipped them with special instincts to help them fly the fastest, surest way. People, too, need direction. God values us so much more than other living things that he wants us to do things in the best possible way. Along with the ability to think and process information, he gives us this promise: "I will instruct you (says the Lord) and guide you along the best pathway for your life; I will advise you and watch your progress" (Psalm 32:8). When we see birds flying in a V formation, looking like an arrow, we should remember that God wants to point the way for us.

## 13

# How did a dead fish help frozen foods flourish?

Clarence Birdseye didn't invent frozen foods—the Eskimos did. But Birdseye came up with a way to make frozen foods taste better after they thaw. While he was working for the government in Labrador, Newfoundland, Birdseye noticed something interesting as he watched Arctic fishermen pull fish out of the water. Soon after the fish hit the 50-degrees-below-zero air, they froze solid. Birdseye figured out that freezing quickly was the secret to good frozen food.

He learned that during the old freezing process, ice crystals damaged food's cells. Juices leaked out, and the food spoiled and turned mushy because it was frozen so slowly. Anyone who had tried to eat these bad-tasting early frozen foods never wanted to try them again. Also, stores were supposed to buy expensive refrigeration equipment. As a result, it was hard to convince people to use frozen foods. Eventually Birdseye sold his business to Postem, which became General Foods. The first thing General Foods did to boost sales was to label the foods "frosted" instead of "frozen." Then they installed free refrigeration units in 18 grocery stores. Consumers didn't have freezers at home, so they had to eat the food the same day it was purchased.

What really made frozen foods popular was World War II. Women were working and didn't have time to cook. Since canned foods used so much metal, which was needed for the war, frozen foods were available for fewer ration coupons. It was even possible to rent space at a food locker to store frozen foods until they were needed. The popularity of frozen foods has grown over the years, and today the Birds Eye brand can be found in virtually every grocery store.

The Eskimos probably weren't even aware that Birdseye was watching them, yet what he saw influenced his entire life's work. You may not have noticed it, but someone may be watching you. If he is trying to copy you, what will he learn? If you'd like to be a good influence but you're not really sure how to go about it, the Bible gives a great tip. It says, "Urge the young men to behave carefully, taking life seriously. And here you yourself must be an example to them of good deeds of every kind. Let everything you do reflect your love of the truth and the fact that you are in dead earnest about it" (Titus 2:6-7). Telling someone what they should do isn't very convincing. We have the power to really make a difference in someone's life by just showing what we know about Jesus.

# 14

# When can books become a bother?

Once there was a man whose goal was to own one copy of every book in the world. In the early 1800s, he came as close as he could. His name was Sir Thomas Phillipps, and he tried to collect every printed paper available, going even so far as to gather other people's trash.

Boxes of books were constantly being delivered to his house. Sir Thomas kept his books in boxes similar to coffins so that they could be moved quickly in case of fire, which he greatly feared. But the books were not organized in any way, so they weren't really usable. They were covered with dust and surrounded by logs, which Sir Thomas hoped would distract the beetles away from eating the covers and pages.

Sir Thomas spent so much time and money on his books that his daughters could only afford to have one dress each, and the family was always near bankruptcy. When the floors of their house began to sag under the weight of all the paper and they needed more room for books, they decided to move.

It took 230 horses, 103 wagons, and 160 men to help move the books to the new house. Even then, some books were left behind, along with the parts of wagons that broke because the books were so heavy. The final tally of Sir Thomas's collection was larger than the Cambridge University library—around 60,000 manuscripts and more than one million books. What happened to all these books after Sir Thomas died? His family was still selling them at auctions a century later.

There was a lot of knowledge available to Sir Thomas in the books he had collected. He was so busy gathering the volumes, however, that he didn't have time to read them. Sometimes we also allow our life to be cluttered with busyness. We don't take time to read the one book that can teach us the most important things we'll ever need to know. We are told, "Search the book of the Lord and see all that he will do; not one detail will he miss" (Isaiah 34:16). If we are using the only free time we can spare to search the newspaper for news, sales, or coupons, we're looking in the wrong place. There's no better source to find good news or more free gifts than in the Bible.

## 15

# How did a medicine bottle turn into a toy?

Childproof bottle caps have saved many young lives. Kunming Corporation, a Chinese pharmaceutical company, may have taken the childproof cap concept a step too far. Their aspirin bottle had 13 separate moving parts, and it took 39 steps to open the cap. If that wasn't enough to deter a child from opening the bottle, the tricky top was replaced with a new model every six months.

The Kunming Corporation received a surprise when they learned why people were buying the baffling bottles. It wasn't because protective parents were hoping to discourage curious little fingers. Rather, the most bottles were bought for children who used the cap as a puzzle to solve.

Challenges can be fun when you're looking for something to keep you busy. Sometimes there are stumbling blocks in life that aren't enjoyable. Maybe you don't know how you're going to get out of debt or find a job or take care of your aging parent. You don't know where to turn or how to solve your problem. You feel that your burdens are too much for you to shoulder alone, and you're right. You need God's help. He says, "In this world you will have trouble. But take heart! I have overcome the world" (John 16:33, NIV). Ask God to walk with you through those troubles. His strength will comfort and support you.

# 16
# Which church leader picked nine pins for bowling?

It is thought that bowling has been around since 5200 B.C., because a stone ball and nine pointed stone pins were found in an Egyptian tomb. Bowling, as we know it today, began in the churches of fourth-century Germany.

"Kegle"s were war clubs set up as the pins. The people would pretend that the pins were the devil. Using a rock or ball, they would try to knock down the pins. If they were successful, it was believed that they were living a good life. If they failed, it meant that they had too many sins in their lives.

The number of pins used in German bowling was anywhere from 3 to 17 until Martin Luther picked the number 9, which we began to use in the United States. The first indoor bowling alley was built of wood in London and dates back to 1450. Before that, the bowling "alley" was just the space between buildings or houses outside.

Bowling balls were first made of stone, then wood, then iron, then rubber. They were just rolled off the palm of the hand until two, and later three, holes were drilled. Eventually bowling was used as a way to gamble, so bowling "nine pins" was made illegal in 1839. Players got around the law by adding an extra pin.

No matter how many times we go bowling, we can't knock evil away. There is only one good defense, and the Bible tells us what it is: "Give yourselves humbly to God. Resist the devil and he will flee from you. And when you draw close to God, God will draw close to you" (James 4:7-8). God will strike down the devil if we call on him for protection.

## 17

# How could treason be committed during dinner?

What could you possibly do at the dinner table that would be considered an act of treason? If you lived in England in the seventeenth century, it was as simple as making a toast. And it wasn't even what you said—it was what you didn't say.

There was a family named Stuart that was banished from England. Some English people thought that the Stuarts should have been the real rulers of their country and that it wasn't fair that they were exiled. So when the people made toasts, they had a secret way of showing their support for the Stuarts.

In those days, tables were set with a water bowl at each place, so that the diners could rinse their fingers. If you were in favor of the Stuarts, as you raised your glass during a toast, you would be careful to hold it over your water bowl. That is how you showed that you were toasting the king "over the water," or across the ocean. Eventually the hidden meaning of the toast was discovered by those who didn't agree. As a result, water bowls were no longer put out on the tables. Even though the tradition of water bowls was brought back in later times, it is still considered an insult to have water bowls on the table when a British king or queen is dining.

A traitor is someone who acts in a way that benefits the enemy. There is no "middle ground"—you're either for or against your country. When a person has Jesus as the Lord of his life, he understands what Jesus meant when he said, "Anyone who is not for me is against me; if he isn't helping me, he is hurting my cause" (Luke 11:23).

Our acts of unkindness can push people away from Jesus because we're viewed as his representatives. When we're not trustworthy, others could become distrustful of God as well. We have many chances each day to be a good representative of Jesus and a good soldier in his army. Even the smallest bit of compassion toward a stranger can end up being the exact invitation he's been needing to join up with Jesus.

# What causes
# bad breath?

There are four main reasons why your breath might be especially unpleasant in the morning.

First, if your teeth have decaying food on or between them, your breath will smell bad. When you chew, talk, and swallow, saliva lubricates your mouth and limits your bad breath, but those are things that we don't do while we sleep. Also, during the night, some of the skin inside your mouth is rubbed off and begins to smell.

Add to this the fact that your stomach, which hasn't been given food to digest in a while, will churn during the night. This stirs up stomach gases that rise to your throat. What you have eaten can also give you bad breath, but not because the odor is in your mouth. When you eat onions or garlic, their oils enter your bloodstream and get deposited in your lungs. When you exhale, your breath will carry the smells of those oils mixed with carbon dioxide.

Mouthwashes can mask but not really eliminate bad breath. Otto M. Dyer was worried that he might not know his breath was bad. So in 1957 he patented what he thought was a great way to test the breath. Dyer made a plastic mold that was small enough to be hidden in the palm. When the user raised his hand to his mouth and coughed, a puff of air would be blown through a vent aimed at the user's nose, allowing him to smell his own breath.

In the big picture, every breath is a good one, even if it doesn't have the sweetest smell. Breath means life. Breathing is such an automatic part of our day, we seldom—if ever—

even think about it. Yet breathing is our most vital function. Fortunately, we aren't responsible for keeping ourselves breathing—that would be an all-consuming task. We wouldn't have time to do anything else. God, as always, anticipated our needs. The Bible tells us, "In his hand is the life of every creature and the breath of all mankind" (Job 12:10, NIV). God is so mighty. He is simultaneously watching over our breathing and the breathing of each creature on earth.

## 19
# Why would two brothers booby-trap their house?

Two grown brothers shared a house in the 1940s. The way the brothers lived, however, was very strange. Their house was filled from floor to ceiling with furniture, rags, newspapers, cardboard boxes, and car parts. The collection even featured 14 pianos, thousands of books, and six United States flags.

One of the brothers, Langley, liked to invent things. He tried to make a car motor that could run the electricity in the house and a vacuum that could clean pianos. The other brother, Homer, had been a lawyer until he was afflicted with a disease that made him blind and nearly paralyzed.

The brothers ended up staying in their house all the time.

They boarded up all the windows and had the water and electricity turned off. Langley went out only at night to get supplies. People made up wild stories about hoarded treasure in the house. After some thieves tried to break in, Langley began making booby traps with all the junk in the house. He rigged wires and ropes so that garbage would fall on anyone who tried to enter.

Finally, neighbors noticed that no one had seen either of the brothers in a long time, and they called the police. The police went into the house and found that the sick brother, Homer, had died in his bed. As they began to clear out the house, they discovered what had happened. Langley had accidentally gotten caught in one of his own booby traps and died. Because he wasn't there to take care of his brother, Homer died, too.

When Langley was lying underneath his own trap, unable to get out, you can imagine how much he must have wanted someone to come along and free him. Sometimes we're caught in a trap of our own making. Maybe it's an addiction or maybe it's a wrong that we don't have the power to make right. We need God's help, and he's standing close by, ready to set us free.

If you haven't already asked God to be a part of your life, that's where to start. You can invite him silently—right now, right where you are—and he will begin immediately to share his power with you. Don't worry if you don't see instantaneous results. God cares for you so much that he uses his limitless knowledge to provide you with a better solution to your problem—a solution that even you couldn't imagine. We can believe in the promise that God will stay with us until "we have escaped like a bird out of the fowler's snare; the snare has been broken, and we have escaped" (Psalm 124:7, NIV).

## 20
# What's up with eyebrows?

What happens when we raise our eyebrows? Unlike animals, which depend more on hearing and smell, humans depend most on seeing. While the animals flare their nostrils or raise their ears to heighten their alertness, we widen our eyes, dilate our pupils, and raise our eyebrows to see more clearly. It's a way our body tries to enhance our protection. Lowering our eyebrows in concentration also is a protection device, because a wrinkled brow makes the eyes' openings smaller. Our eyebrows also move because we have learned to communicate by making expressions with our face. Raised eyebrows can show surprise, questioning, disapproval, and interest.

Almost all of us have someone we disapprove of. We don't like the way they talk or act or look. But we shouldn't be too quick to "raise our eyebrows" in scorn at this person. When we think we're better than someone else, we can get into serious trouble. The Bible tells us, "The day is coming when your proud looks will be brought low; the Lord alone will be exalted. On that day the Lord Almighty will move against the proud and haughty and bring them to the dust" (Isaiah 2:11-12). If we don't enjoy having someone look down on us, we shouldn't look down on anyone else. We will be recognized for our goodness when we get to heaven, and that will last a lot longer than being a "high brow" here on earth.

---

## 21
# How do you build a skyscraper with matchsticks?

The first skyscraper was built from matchsticks and playing cards—at least in the architect's mind. In the late 1800s William LeBaron Jenney finally solved the problem of how to build a structure with more than 10 stories. Until then, builders had found that using brick walls would work only up to nine stories. The 10th story caused the whole building to crumble under its own weight. Jenney thought for months about how to overcome this puzzle but without success.

While relaxing, stacking matchsticks to make small boxes, he had an intriguing idea. Jenney covered his matchstick houses with playing cards and realized that this same process, using different materials, might be his answer. If he relied on steel beams for support and then added the bricks, the buildings might be strong enough to be built higher.

Following this blueprint, Jenney oversaw construction of

the first skyscraper in 1885, which went up in Chicago. The skyscraper was only 10 stories high, but it was the addition of that elusive tenth floor that allowed Jenney to prove that he could take buildings to new heights.

If your office ended up being located in the first sky-scraper, you would have to trust that the architect knew what he was doing. You would be going on faith that he hadn't made any mistakes. God wants you to treat him that way, also. He doesn't make mistakes, and he always knows what he's doing. In addition, he is only interested in doing what is good for you. Trust God and have faith in his grand design. The Bible promises that "the name of the Lord is a strong tower; the righteous run to it and are safe" (Proverbs 18:10, NIV).

## 22
# What really makes a bull charge at a red cape?

When a matador flashes a red cape in front of a bull, he's conducting a well-orchestrated "special effects" show. Afterwards, you might worry about wearing a red shirt or taking a red tablecloth on a picnic anywhere near where cattle roam. The matador would be proud that he caused such anxiety. That's because the red cape is for our benefit, not the bull's.

When we see the color red, our blood pressure rises and our pulse speeds up. Red inspires us to have heightened awareness because it is the color of blood, and blood is usually a sign of trouble or danger. The bull doesn't care about the color red. Bulls can't see color—they're color-blind. The reason the bull charges at the matador is not because his cape is red but because the cape is moving. Wave anything—in any color—at a bull, and he will get angry.

If the bull could only control his instincts and think, he could look ahead and figure out that being angry would be a big mistake. Showing anger ends in death by the mata-dor's sword. If the bull could refuse to get upset, it's entirely possible that the matador would choose another bull that would put on a better show for the crowds.

But bulls can't reason as we can. God gave us the ability to exert power over our impulses by using our brains. That is why the Bible tells us, "A wise man controls his temper. He knows that anger causes mistakes" (Proverbs 14:29). Refusing to be angry is a choice, and the more often we avoid anger, the less likely we'll be to find ourselves face-to-face with a sword in the center of the ring.

## 23

# How did a Christmas card lead to a unique advertising campaign?

Clinton Odell heard of a chemist who had become ill and moved to Arizona for his health. Clinton sent $25 and an encouraging note to the chemist at Christmastime. A year later, in 1925, the chemist, Carl Noren, appeared at the Odell house saying, "I'm here and I'm well, and what can I do for you?" That was the beginning of Burma-Shave.

Clinton asked Carl if he knew anything about brushless shaving cream, which he thought would be a good idea because men wouldn't have to pack their wet brushes in their suitcases anymore. Carl mixed up Batch #1 and was working on Batch "Almost 300" when Clinton found a little bit of leftover Batch #43 and shaved with it. He liked it and realized that it worked because it had aged for a few months.

Now he had a good product to advertise. Clinton's son, Allan, saw some gas station road signs that followed one another on the roadside, telling of gas, oil, and rest rooms. These signs gave him the idea for Burma-Shave's new campaign. With a $200 budget, the family painted crude, unrhymed signs, hurrying to hammer them into the ground before it froze. Then repeat orders started coming in from druggists whose customers traveled the two roads where the signs had been distributed.

The signs had several advantages: It took almost 18 seconds to read a series of them, which was more time than most advertisers could expect to get from their readers. Also, the separated signs created suspense because there was no way to "cheat" by skipping ahead to the ending. The signs also used humor, and rhyming was eventually added, which delighted readers. Some examples of these innovative signs are: "The bearded lady / Tried a jar / She's now / A famous / Movie star / Burma-Shave." "Avoid the store / Which claims / You should / Buy something else / That's just as good / Burma-Shave." "Fisherman! / For a lucky strike / Show the pike / A face / They'll like / Burma-Shave." "If you dislike / Big traffic fines / Slow down / Till you / Can read these signs / Burma-Shave."

One sign provided the Odells with surprising feedback. It said: "Rip a fender / Off your car / Send it in / For a half-pound jar." The Odells received tiny fenders from toy cars, but they also received crates with real fenders packed in them! As promised, everybody got his or her free jar of Burma-Shave.

As you travel the road of life, there will be times when you will wish that you could see some signs telling you how to make things better. The highway sometimes will be dark and rough. You won't have any idea where it will end or what twists and turns await you. But during those moments, don't despair. Even when you're not aware of it, Jesus will be beside you.

Talk to him. Believe in his ability to show you the way. Trust. He will not let you down. He will lead you, and you will become aware of his presence. When you have passed through the rocky places, you will be able to look back and say to him with certainty, "Your word is a lamp to my feet and a light for my path" (Psalm 119:105, NIV). Turn on the light by turning to Jesus.

## 24

# What can you do with a useless tunnel?

When you're working on a project, it's tempting to get sidetracked. But perhaps no one was more distracted than a man called William Henry "Burro" Schmidt. Schmidt was born in Rhode Island but went to California when he was 24 to prospect for gold. He was fortunate and struck gold. Before he began to work his claim, however, Schmidt got off track. He reasoned that he shouldn't begin mining his gold until he had built a tunnel through Copper Mountain. Then he could transport his gold directly to the road on the other side, to the smelter, where the gold would be purified.

Schmidt began digging his tunnel, using just hand tools and occasionally dynamite. He worked alone, except for the company of his two burros, Jack and Jenny, which is how he got the nickname "Burro." For the next 43 years, Burro dug, often in the dark, because there was not enough air in the tunnel for a candle to stay lit.

Ironically, all around him progress was taking place quickly. A road was built over the mountain, and railroad tracks were also installed. But Burro had set out to build his tunnel, and he wasn't going to quit. Finally at the age of 67, Burro reached the other side of the mountain.

But what can you do with an obsolete, hand-dug tunnel? You can open it to the public as a tourist attraction, which is what Burro did for the next 16 years until his death. He had earned for his efforts a second nickname: "The Human Mole," given to him by Robert Ripley of "Believe It or Not" fame.

Even though Burro Schmidt may not have picked the most productive project, he has to be admired for his tenacity. Once he got the tunnel idea in his head, absolutely nothing could stop him from finishing the task. That's the kind of devotion that God would like to see in us. He promises, "He who endures to the end will be saved" (Matthew 24:13, RSV). Learn from Burro's commitment. With the Bible as our guide, we'll never need to worry about whether or not we're working on doing the right thing. We will be, so we should feel free to do it with all our might.

## 25
# Why leave your business card when you don't even work?

When you hand someone your business card, it probably states who you are and what kind of business you're in. You're hoping that this person will need your services or will pass your name along to someone else who might. Handing out cards is one way of advertising and marketing yourself.

Business cards are not a new idea. They have been used since before World War I. Only the purpose is different. Long ago the only people who had cards were upper-crust, old-moneyed gentry. They left their cards at any house they visited, which is how they spent much of their time—going from home to home, making it apparent that they weren't working because they didn't need to. At that time leaving your card was an exercise in social etiquette. Then the twentieth century dawned, and people began to feel that visiting for visiting's sake was a waste of time. For a while, into the early 1960s, name cards were used for both purposes, but not long thereafter, the business card survived, and the calling card became all but extinct.

Calling cards were the old way and dropped out to make way for the new. That's how it is when you become a follower of Jesus. The worn-out, tattered person that you used to be fades away. You will develop instead a freshness of perspective, strength, and hope. Jesus says, "Behold, I make all things new" (Revelation 21:5, RSV). Trash that outdated "calling card" personality that's been keeping you distraught and discouraged. Trade it in for a new "card" that shows you're in the business of new beginnings.

# 26
## How did a tomato create an emergency by calling 9-1-1?

Something was wrong.

The emergency switchboard in Blacksburg, Virginia, received a 9-1-1 call, but no one on the other end said anything. Then a second call came in, also completely silent. Several similar calls followed. The call was traced to Linda and Danny Hurst's home. Sheriff's deputies had no idea what kind of a situation would be waiting for them as they raced to the Hurst house. Guns drawn, they approached the residence. All seemed quiet. Further inspection showed that the Hursts weren't home, and no one else seemed to be there, either. There was no evidence of burglary or foul play.

How were the 9-1-1 calls being placed? The deputies finally solved the riddle. Near the telephone and answering machine, they found a basket. And in the basket was a tomato that had become mushy and dripped on the machinery, causing a short that resulted in the 9-1-1 calls.

It's good to know that we can call 9-1-1 and get a quick response—even a tomato can get an answer! It should be much more important to us to know that we can get an answer from God when we call for his help, too. Jesus said, about God his Father, that "you can ask him for anything, using my name, and I will do it, for this will bring praise to the Father because of what I, the Son, will do for you. Yes, ask anything, using my name, and I will do it!" (John 14:13-14). We don't even need a phone line, because we have a prayer line. We should use it all the time—not only when there's a crisis.

## 27

# What can you do with a pack of camels?

The United States gained a half-million square miles of land after the war with Mexico. The land was like a desert and didn't even have a railway to help deliver goods. Americans who had visited the Middle East thought that using camels to cross the desert would be a good idea.

Camels can close their ears and noses to keep out blowing sand and have two rows of eyelashes to protect their eyes. Camels can go a week without water, travel as many as 40 miles in a single day, and carry a thousand pounds. Congress voted to buy 76 camels in 1856. The camels came from Egypt and Turkey and arrived in Texas. The army was going to use the camels to move soldiers and supplies into the new desert territory. That's when the problems began. Soldiers were afraid of the camels, and so was every horse in the vicinity. The Turkish veterinarian hired to take care of the camels had no training. His method for curing a camel was to tickle its nose with a chameleon's tail. Soon it became obvious that the United States just wasn't prepared for the camel plan.

The idea was good, but the results were disastrous. After a while the Civil War started, and the army packed up the camel idea. But what could be done with the camels? Someone had the idea that the camels could be used for delivering mail—a "Camel Express"! That wasn't practical either for the same reasons that the army couldn't use the camels. Eventually the camels were delivered, without mail, to circuses and zoos.

Whenever something is too heavy for us to carry alone, we look around for help. Even though these particular camels couldn't be used as workers, people have long depended on camels as beasts of burden. Unfortunately, camels can't carry some of the heaviest burdens we encounter—like illness or anger or sorrow. God does not expect us to shoulder these weights by ourselves, however. The Bible tells us, "Give your burdens to the Lord. He will carry them" (Psalm 55:22). One of the blessings of asking God into your life is the assurance that you won't be facing anything alone ever again. God will be with you whenever you cross a spiritual desert, lightening your load with his comfort.

---

## 28
# How were Life Savers saved?

Even though Edward Noble didn't invent Life Savers, he is the reason that we still enjoy them today. Noble's job was to advertise products. He bought the Life Saver invention from Clarence Crane because he thought that Life

Savers could be a big success. He was wrong at first. Noble found out that the mint Life Savers did not stay fresh in their paper tubes. To make things worse, the candy even began to taste like paper. Anyone who bought a pack of Life Savers didn't want to try them again. Noble made a tinfoil wrapper, but people still said, "No, thank you!"

How could Life Savers get a second chance? Noble asked store owners to put Life Savers in a special place next to the cash registers with a sign that said Five Cents. In addition, Noble asked store owners to be sure to include a nickel whenever a customer got change at the register. Because the customers had the right price of the candy in their hands, they began to try Life Savers again.

Not only were they eating Life Savers, but people began using the candy in creative ways, such as decorations for a Christmas tree or holders for candles on a birthday cake. Noble had invented a new way of selling. People bought so many Life Savers that other companies wanted to put their products near the cash register, too. Soon, Life Savers were getting lost among all the other products near the cash register. Noble got another idea. He built a special rack for holding all kinds of candy and put his Life Savers right up front. The next time you see a candy rack near the register, you'll likely notice that Life Savers are the first in line.

The only true "Lifesaver" is Jesus, and he is offering the sweet gift of salvation. The Bible makes this very clear and simple. It says, "Whoever has God's Son has life; whoever does not have his Son, does not have life" (1 John 5:12). If you were drowning and someone threw a lifeline or an inflated tube to you, you'd grab it and not let go. God is offering you his Son. Clutch him to your heart and hang on for dear life.

# Why are a cat's whiskers better than a man's?

A man's whiskers can keep his face warm in the winter and change his appearance. If he shaves them off, all he loses is some hair. But cats depend on their whiskers for survival. Cut them off, and you could cripple the cat's ability to take care of itself. That's because the cat uses its whiskers to judge distances. The whiskers stick out from the cat's cheeks, upper lip, and forehead. The cat has very sensitive nerves where the whiskers meet skin. When something brushes against the tips of the whiskers, the cat's face feels it. Cats can tell from their whisker "antennae" how far away something is, which is important for an animal that pads around in the dark. If its whiskers are touching both sides of an opening, the cat can tell that the rest of its body won't fit through, and it avoids getting stuck.

If we were in charge of creating an animal like the cat, would we have had the foresight to equip that animal with such a helpful type of "curb feelers"? Probably not. God thought of a very creative way to allow the cat to protect itself. The cat is just one of the animals to which God gave amazing abilities. Nature is full of wonderful examples of God's planning. Taking the time to notice them will help us realize "how many are your works, O Lord! In wisdom you made them all" (Psalm 104:24, NIV).

# 30

# Why do all movie scenes start with that black-and-white clapboard?

"Quiet on the set," yells the director as the black-and-white-striped board is raised, clicked, and removed. The movie scene begins. As familiar as this process may be, the reason for using the clapboard is not as well known.

Writing on the board tells filmmakers which scene is being filmed and how many times it has been repeated. Why, then, is it necessary to snap the hinged pieces together at each beginning? It has to do with matching the sound to the actions in a movie. It's important that actors' mouths move at exactly the same time as their words are spoken.

The clapperboard is a way to test the sound. It is always shut as soon as the cameras start to roll so that sound technicians can use this noise for reference. They make sure that the snapping of the clapboard is heard when the closing of the hinge is shown. This adjusts the rest of the sounds in the scene so that they, too, will be heard at the precise time.

Some time or another we all feel like we're out of sync, like we're not matching up with the rest of the world. When we speak, no one seems to understand what we're trying to say. When we act, the results don't come out the way we expected. If you're frustrated and discouraged, call on God to direct your life. He will be glad to take action. The Bible says, "Lord, it is time for you to act" (Psalm 119:126). God's timing is never wrong. When you need a boost, he will help you find the right pace again.

———————————————— 31

# When can colors be confusing?

More males than females suffer from color blindness. One out of every 12 men and one out of every 200 women are color-blind. Color blindness may be hereditary and reveals itself in several variations. Some people have trouble distinguishing between yellow and green or red and green because these colors appear gray. People who are completely color-blind see only shades of black and white. There are people who aren't even aware of their color blindness. They think that the gray they're seeing is called "red" and that everyone else is seeing gray, too. As for animals, tests have shown that dogs and cats are completely color-blind. Horses, bees, and monkeys can distinguish between some colors, and hens can tell all colors apart.

There are different ways to use your eyes to "see" regardless of your ability to distinguish colors. One kind of sight helps you to learn about the world. The other kind of sight helps you to understand and comprehend. God wants us to use our vision to do both for him. He says, "You will seek me and find me when you seek me with all your heart" (Jeremiah 29:13, NIV). Search for God in Scripture and in the world. He will open your eyes to new understanding.

# 32
# Why did some coffins have alarms?

The fear of being buried alive is very real for many people. An invention called the Life Detector could keep you alive until rescuers arrived—if you happened to come back to life in your coffin. A machine, like the ones used in hospitals to monitor vital signs, was attached to an alarm and an oxygen-activating device. If you showed any signs of life, the alarm went off, and oxygen flowed.

During Victorian times, people were buried with shovels and crowbars so they could dig themselves out. There were tubes coming up through the ground in case the deceased awoke and needed to yell for help. Wealthy people sometimes hired servants to stay near the pipes and listen. A bell might be put on top of the coffin, with the rope placed in the dead person's hand so that if he awoke, he could summon help. Coffins have even been equipped with electric buzzers.

Many people felt that they had to protect themselves *before* they ended up in the coffin. Hans Christian Anderson, the children's book author, took several precautions. In his pocket he carried a card that specified that he was to be examined by a physician before being presumed dead. In addition, whenever he slept, he placed a sign nearby that read, "I only seem dead." This preoccupation with death extended even so far as to motivate Henry Ford to capture Thomas Edison's dying breath in a bottle and save it until his own death 16 years later.

We sometimes feel overconfident about our ability to direct every aspect of our life. We want to be "in control." But we are not in charge—God is. The Bible reminds us of our lack of power when it asks, "Who of you by worrying can add a single hour to his life?" (Matthew 6:27, NIV). We are not to worry but to trust. God knows the right time for us to join him in heaven. Until then, he wants us to be concerned about helping others instead of working uselessly to preserve ourselves.

# 33

# How did clay flowerpots help make buildings better?

Joseph Monier was trying to make a bigger flowerpot, but he learned how to build a bridge instead. He was a commercial gardener who was having trouble making large flowerpots with clay. In 1849 he thought of covering some wire netting with concrete. He was very pleased with the results.

Then he began thinking of other uses for his concrete. He tried iron bars instead of wire netting and realized that large construction structures, like bridges and dams, could be built stronger. What made Monier's idea so valuable was that bars alone, or concrete alone, were not as strong as when the two were combined. As an added bonus, the iron bars didn't even rust when they were covered in concrete. Monier patented his idea, which provided a better way to build.

Clay or cement, without mesh, can't withstand too much pressure and crumbles easily. Maybe you've been feeling a little like that lately. You're under quite a bit of pressure—worried that sooner or later you're going to crack or fall apart. Fortify yourself by asking God to help you. Nothing is too much for him to handle, and he invites you to come to him when you are weak. He says, "My grace is sufficient for thee: for my strength is made perfect in weakness" (2 Corinthians 12:9, KJV). Ask God to be the iron in your structure, and together you will form an indestructible combination.

# 34

# What did a touch tell in trial?

Early courtroom justice involved some fairly strange procedures. "Trials by touch," for example, were popular in America during the seventeenth century. The defendant was ordered to touch the body of the deceased victim. If the corpse moved or changed in any way, it was interpreted by the court as a sign of guilt—the victim's objection to being touched by the murderer.

In China the defendant was given a mouthful of rice to prove his innocence or guilt. If he could swallow the rice, the verdict was innocent. The Chinese believed that a guilty person, who was usually nervous and had a dry mouth, wouldn't be able to swallow the rice.

Does the evidence in your life identify you as a follower of Jesus Christ? Would a judge and jury find enough evidence that you are obeying God's command to love your neighbor as yourself? If not, how could you exhibit this love to those around you?

The Bible gives us a checklist: "Love is very patient and kind, never jealous or envious, never boastful or proud, never haughty or selfish or rude. Love does not demand its own way. It is not irritable or touchy. It does not hold grudges and will hardly even notice when others do it wrong. It is never glad about injustice, but rejoices whenever truth wins out. If you love someone, you will be loyal to him no matter what the cost. You will always believe in him, always expect the best of him, and always stand your ground in defending him" (1 Corinthians 13:4-7). Let Jesus "touch" your life, and you will get a life sentence in heaven!

## 35

# What's the big secret behind Betty Crocker?

Most of us are familiar with her or have at least heard her name—the happy, competent cook and homemaker known as Betty Crocker. Her radio show, *The Betty Crocker Cooking School of the Air*, debuted in 1924, continued for 24 years, and had more than one million listeners. Betty Crocker has served as the official home-baker's guide by answering letters to cooking questions and has sold more than 50 million cookbooks. One ingredient is missing, however, from her secret recipe for success—she's entirely made up. There has never been a person named Betty Crocker.

It all started in 1921. The Washburn Crosby Company of Minneapolis was getting hundreds of letters each week from women who wanted baking advice. In an attempt to give their responses a personal touch, the company, which later became part of General Mills, invented a lady to answer the mail. "Crocker" was her last name in honor of a retired company director, William Crocker. "Betty" was chosen because the name sounded friendly.

A secretary's handwriting won the company contest to create a signature for the fictitious female. When the radio show began, Betty Crocker needed a voice, so an actress was hired. Fifteen years later a picture was needed for the cookbooks. A composite portrait was painted from all of the women employees. The picture was updated in 1955, 1965, 1980, and again in the 1990s. Each version made Betty appear progressively younger. For someone who never existed, Betty Crocker accomplished a great deal.

No one had ever heard of Betty Crocker before 1921, and even after that, they only saw a picture, never a person. People were convinced that she really existed because they knew what she "said" in her books and radio shows. It's amazing that people have known for centuries what Jesus said in the Bible, but they still resist him because they haven't seen him with their own eyes. Why is it easier to accept a conjured-up cook than it is to acknowledge a real-life Savior? Jesus says, "Blessed are those who haven't seen me and believe anyway" (John 20:29).

---

## 36
# What sent the price of raccoon tails climbing?

What sent the price of raccoon tails zooming from 25¢ to $8 a pound and caused children to run around with bows and arrows, moccasins, and rubber knives? Davy Crockett had arrived on the scene. In 1954 Walt Disney Studios aired a one-hour television program called *Davy Crockett, Indian Fighter.* It was the first installment of a three-part series, and no one, including Walt Disney himself, expected it to be very popular. But children loved the show, and a merchandising bonanza began.

Before the year was over, the Davy Crockett theme song had been recorded by 17 different artists, and Crockett's picture was plastered on lunch boxes, jigsaw puzzles, comic books, baby shoes, tablets, and anything else that could bear printing. The most easily identified symbol of the Disney show was the raccoon cap worn by Crockett. In all, souvenir sales totaled more than $100 million.

Children love to imitate what's popular. The Davy Crockett craze, for example, and the desire to do what everyone else is doing are harmless up to a point. We've probably all been asked as children, or have had occasion to ask our own kids, that infamous question, "Would you jump off a cliff just because your friends did?" Part of becoming an adult involves deciding whether your boss, mentor, or peers are leading you in the best possible direction. It is difficult to entrust your life to someone as you grow older because you realize that most people are as frail and fallible as you are.

There is only one true guide for your life. Jesus says, "I am the Light of the world. So if you follow me, you won't be stumbling through the darkness, for living light will flood your path" (John 8:12). You don't have to question your security or your well-being when you choose to follow Jesus. He never lies, he will never betray you, and he will always lead you to do the right thing. If you're saying to yourself, "Somebody would have to be superhuman to live up to that description," you're exactly right!

# How are crossword puzzles connected with Christmas?

The first crossword puzzle was published in a small newspaper, *The New York World,* by Arthur Wynne for the 1913 Christmas edition. Wynne wanted something a little different for the issue, so he made a diamond-shaped puzzle that was similar to the one he remembered his grandfather showing him. The readers loved Wynne's "word-cross."

Railroad commuters in the 1920s became the crossword puzzle's biggest fans—so much so that dictionaries were provided on trains, and crosswords were even printed on the backs of dining-car menus. In England, librarians blacked out copies of the crosswords so fanatical patrons would return their newspapers. Germans even dropped pamphlets over England during World War II that had crosswords containing propagandized clues: The clue for "Churchill" was "warmonger."

Crossword puzzles also gave a well-respected publishing firm its start. Simon and Schuster's first book, *The Crossword Puzzle Book,* began with a $75 advance and sold 123,000 copies. It was available by mail order in 1924 for $1.35. A true indication of how crossword-crazy people became was the minister who challenged his congregation to complete a crossword puzzle pertaining to his sermon.

Crossword puzzles give clues. It's your job to fill in the spaces with the word that you think the clue is describing. Here's a clue for you and the answer has five spaces: "Look! I have been standing at the door, and I am constantly knocking. If anyone hears me calling him and opens the door, I will come in and fellowship with him and he with me" (Revelation 3:20).

Can you figure out who thinks you're so special that he continuously stands outside your door, knocking and calling your name, and waiting patiently for you to answer? He won't enter without an invitation but wants you to know that he's ready to meet you anytime and give you gifts of peace, hope, and encouragement. Could you "fill in the blank" with the name of any friend of yours? No human could love you as much as this "mystery guest." Who is it? Open the door and see for yourself—his name is J-E-S-U-S.

# 38

# Why did farmers have curfews?

The concept of a curfew dates back to medieval times when farmers would keep a fire burning out in the fields or woods to stay warm in the winter. The fire was supposed to be put out after the day's chores were finished for safety's sake. But sometimes the farmers forgot and an out-of-control fire would destroy everything in its path. A law was passed that required all open fires to be covered up at dusk.

A bell would ring from the village church to remind everyone to *couvre-feu*. In French, this means "cover fire" and sounds similar to what we pronounce as "curfew." The British, who thought *couvre-feu* was a good idea, began to use the custom in their country and changed the spelling of the word. Eventually, the curfew came to mean the time when anyone should stop what they're doing and go home.

Most of us don't like being cold and in the dark. When darkness comes, we naturally gravitate toward the warmth of the light. Our souls are no different. When we are chilled by dark feelings of hopelessness, helplessness, or despair, we long to see a flame's flicker. The Bible offers words of encouragement and invitation by teaching us about God. It says, "His life is the light that shines through the darkness—and the darkness can never extinguish it" (John 1:5). Don't settle for a small spark when you're discouraged. Remember that you have access to a bonfire!

## 39
# Where were houses built roof-first and books read back to front?

The Chinese culture contains a long, rich history of traditions and customs that in some cases might seem opposite to the ones we know. Until the modernization of China (and to some extent still today), when Chinese people met someone, they shook their own hand instead of their new acquaintance's. China had "lending libraries" on the curbs, where children who couldn't afford to buy comic books could rent them long enough to sit by the booth and read them. Letters were addressed with the destination written on the top line and the person's name written at the bottom of the envelope. It was acceptable to put the saucer on top of the teacup, instead of beneath it, in order to keep the tea warm. Books started at the back and ended in the front. Houses were built roof-first.

Every country, as well as every generation, has its own customs. We owe much of what we know to our ancestors, who carefully passed on to us what experience had taught them. The Bible tells us of our greatest heritage: "Understand, therefore, that the Lord your God is the faithful God who for a thousand generations keeps his promises and constantly loves those who love him and who obey his commands" (Deuteronomy 7:9). Start a custom of your own by passing on the legacy of God's love to someone else. It will be a lifesaving experience.

# Why did a priest decide to live with lepers?

It takes a very special person to devote his entire life to the service of others. Father Damien was one of those special people. From early adolescence, Joseph (Father Damien's given name until he became a priest) was good at many tasks. He served his community as a painter, schoolteacher, cook, gardener, carpenter, and even doctor—whatever was needed. He and his brother studied together to become priests. Joseph's brother wanted to be a missionary, but he wasn't strong enough to work because of health problems.

At 22, Joseph was ordained as "Father Damien." He decided to serve as a missionary in his brother's place and spent the next 10 years in the South Sea Islands. He then volunteered to run a leper colony on the Hawaiian island of Molokai. Leprosy was believed to be highly contagious, although it is currently considered no more contagious than the common cold and is completely curable. At that time, however, not many people were willing to visit, much less live in isolation with, the lepers. The priest helped change the squalid, neglected colony into a tidy, pleasant village.

Father Damien eventually contracted the disease after living with the lepers for 10 years. On the last Sunday he was alive, the Gospel reading for the day was "I am the Good Shepherd. The Good Shepherd lays down his life for the sheep" (John 10:11). Father Damien is mentioned in history because he followed Jesus with his whole heart, soul, mind, and body in an attempt to be a "good shepherd."

Not everyone can serve God to the same degree as Father Damien. But we can look for opportunities to serve in our own ways. Say some words of encouragement to a coworker. Smile at your children and hug them more often. Read to someone in a nursing home. Jesus laid his life down for us. If we follow him, God will be pleased by our efforts to nurture the "flock."

# 41

# Who served as president for only one day?

If you could be president of the United States for a day, what would you try to accomplish? David Rice Atchison had that opportunity in 1849.

It was time to swear in the new president, Zachary Taylor. Inauguration day fell on a Sunday, but Taylor didn't want to be sworn in until Monday. President James K. Polk officially concluded his duties on Saturday, which left Sunday, March 4, as a day without a president. The only way to fill the vacancy was to have the next in line, President Pro Tem David Atchison of the Senate, take over for that day.

Did Senator Atchison make a big difference to our country on that day? Hardly. He was exhausted from finishing all the business in Congress from President Polk's last day. On

Saturday night, very late, he finally went home to sleep. President Atchison spent his entire one-day term in bed, snoring away.

Senator Atchison missed a once-in-a-lifetime chance of having the power and doing the work of the president of the United States. It pales in comparison, though, to having God's power behind us and doing his work. We have that opportunity every day. Jesus said, "As long as it is day, we must do the work of him who sent me" (John 9:4, NIV). You've been authorized to become God's representative today—will you take charge?

## 42
# Which author was always tempted by risky investments?

If you've ever made an investment that didn't turn out exactly right, don't feel alone. Mark Twain, author of *Tom Sawyer* and *Huckleberry Finn*, spent part of his life trying to regain what he lost in one investment.

In theory, the idea was great. It was a typesetting machine that could set type three times faster than a human. It would be another 50 years before its achievements were duplicated again. The inventor, James W. Paige, offered Twain half interest in the machine if the author would provide even more money above his initial $13,000 investment. Paige talked him into another $30,000.

But Paige was always thinking of another way to improve his machine, and he used up all the money. Eventually, Twain provided $3,000 and then $4,000 each month—always in return for a promise from Paige of a finished invention in a few days. Twain was running out of money. Instead of writing, he was pursuing other investors to help with expenses.

Once, he found a millionaire who said he would invest $100,000 if he could see the machine, which was now working beautifully. By the time Twain took the millionaire for a demonstration, the machine was in pieces all over the floor. Paige had decided to make yet another improvement at the last minute. A successful machine was eventually introduced to the public, but it was so complicated that only Paige could make any adjustments. Twain lost $190,000.

Only two machines were ever built. One was donated to a World War II scrap-metal drive. The other one is in the Mark Twain memorial. It took Twain three years of constant lectures and writing to pay back his creditors, which he did, down to the last dollar. Within a month, however, Twain was ready to invest in another new invention, and it was only his business manager who kept him from repeating the costly experience.

Mark Twain did the honorable thing by paying back the people who had loaned him money. Did you know that God wants you to stay in debt? He's not talking about money, though. The Bible says, "Pay all your debts except the debt of love for others—never finish paying that!" (Romans 13:8).

# When can you strike a nerve at the dentist's office?

The dentist offers you an injection of Novocain, an anesthetic, but you're afraid. How will you be able to warn the dentist when he's hitting the nerve of your tooth if you can't feel anything? Furthermore, you worry that if he does drill, he will damage the nerve, and then you'll need even more extensive work done on your tooth.

Do you really need to be so guarded and anxious? No. When you experience pain as the dentist works on your tooth, chances are very good that he's nowhere near the nerve. The most sensitive part of your tooth is where the enamel (the hard coating on your tooth) and the dentin (the tissue directly underneath the enamel) meet. If you told the dentist to stop there, he wouldn't be able to work on your tooth at all.

It's very stressful to be "on guard" all the time. There are so many situations to protect yourself from during the course of each day. Sometimes, you're so busy looking out for dangers that you don't have time to do anything else. You experience frustration because you're not being constructive or productive. You're distracted, cynical, and suspicious all the time. This is no way to live.

If you could, you'd love to hire someone to protect you from these threats to your heart and soul, in the same way that you would hire a bodyguard to watch out for your physical well-being. There is good news. You can have protection for your soul, and it's free for the asking. Each time you feel afraid, repeat to yourself: "God is my defense" (Psalm 59:9, KJV). He is always alert on your behalf and will use his almighty power to defeat your fears, which have become your enemy. Don't let fear steal your peace of mind or your concentration. Instead, trust that God will clear your path so that you can continue to make positive contributions in his name.

## 44
# Where does dew come from if it doesn't fall?

Most of us see dew on the grass in the morning, and we imagine it falling softly during the night when we weren't looking. But dew doesn't "fall" at all. It comes from the air but not like rain. Most of the time air holds water vapor. At night, when the temperature cools down, the air can't continue to hold its moisture.

A blade of grass, as it gets cooler, also cools the blanket of air surrounding it. When the air reaches a certain low temperature, called the "dew point," water from the air condenses onto the grass blade. But not all moisture on the grass is officially dew. The grass also draws water from the soil, and this moisture is pushed out through the blades. It would be possible to notice the process all day long except that the heat of the day causes droplets to evaporate before they're completely formed.

Grass needs moisture to live, and so do we. Have you ever been so thirsty that even a swallow of liquid would be a real treat? God understands our physical needs. He uses the idea of thirst to let us know how abundantly he will bless us—not just with a drop or a swallow, but beyond our every expectation.

He says, "I will give you abundant water for your thirst and for your parched fields. And I will pour out my Spirit and my blessings on your children. They shall thrive like watered grass, like willows on a riverbank (Isaiah 44:3-4). When you are God's child, he knows your needs, both body and soul. Count on him to nourish your soul with his constant flowing love.

## 45

# What's the spin on revolving doors?

As you push your way through a revolving door, do you ever wonder why it's there? It's not used for counting people or to keep them from crowding together through the doorway. So what is its purpose? And why do some buildings have revolving doors, while others don't?

The revolving door's only purpose is to conserve energy—not yours, but the building's. The air pressure outside of a building is different than the air pressure inside, in the same way that the temperature is different. This difference causes air to gush from the inside to the outside, or vice versa, whenever a regular door is opened.

When cold air flows in, the building's furnace tries to warm it up. When hot air flows in, the building's air conditioner tries to cool it down. The building doesn't know that the blast of air is only temporary, and energy is wasted as it adjusts to the new air. A revolving door never lets a clear strong gust of air into the building, so there's no change in air pressure, no gust of wind, no change of temperature, and no waste of energy.

Children seem fascinated with revolving doors. They will deliberately pass by the opening into the building just to keep pushing the door around in a circle. But there are times when going around in circles isn't so fun. Maybe each time you try to break a bad habit, you slip back into your old ways. Or as soon as you put a little extra money aside, your car needs an overhaul. Or the faster you get your job done, the more work you receive.

When you begin to feel that there is no way out of life's revolving door, listen to Jesus. He says, "I am the way and the truth and the life. No one comes to the Father except through me" (John 14:6, NIV). When we open our heart to Jesus, all of our challenges will not disappear. Only through him, however, do we have the assurance that he will lead us through our troubles and take us safely through the door to eternal life.

# How did the tuxedo get its name?

Griswold Lorillard didn't like dressing up in formal attire to attend parties. In fact, he didn't even care who knew about his objection to the traditional white swallow-tailed coat. That's why, in 1886, Griswold arrived at a New York country club wearing a special dinner jacket, thought to have been designed by his father, who had the same aversion.

Griswold's dinner jacket resembled the formal smoking jacket worn in Great Britain. It was considered too casual, however, to be worn in the presence of ladies since it was missing long tails in back, was black in color, and had satin lapels. The jacket was such a contrast to every other man's outfit, it shocked all the guests at the party. They never expected anyone to defy convention by wearing something so informal.

Nevertheless, there must have been many gentlemen who secretly agreed with Griswold. The new dinner jacket caught on and eventually became the accepted formal style for men. Griswold's jacket even got an American name of its own, from the place where it was first worn. The party took place in Tuxedo Park, New York.

It's amazing how much excitement was caused by the appearance of a mere dinner jacket. Imagine, then, how astonished the country clubbers would have been had God caught their attention instead of a garment. The Bible describes him for us: "O Lord my God, how great you are! You are robed with honor and with majesty and light!" (Psalm 104:1). If you're paying less attention to the condition of your soul than to the condition of your clothes, it's time to borrow from God's closet. When your soul is clothed in his light, your inner glow will add dazzle and style to whatever outfit you wear.

# 47

# Why do we drive on the right side of the road?

Although no one seems to know for sure, it appears that shields, wagons, and horsewhips are three historical reasons we drive on the right side of the road in America. In Roman times, soldiers carried their shields in their left hands, so they always tried to pass strangers on the right. Later, teams of wagon horses were led by the right hand as the man walked in front of them. He wanted passing wagons to be on his left, so he could make sure the horses didn't get too close.

During the days of the covered wagon, which rarely had front seats, the driver sat on the back of the animal at the left rear. Since the driver was usually right-handed, sitting far to the left allowed him to manipulate the whip more easily and reach all the animals. In addition, he often carried a rifle crooked in his left arm, aimed toward the left, so the trigger could be fired quickly with his right hand. Because the driver could see the wagon wheels better on the left side of his wagon, he could make sure that his wheels didn't lock with another wagon's if he kept his own to the right.

People need to be attentive when they're driving. It's necessary to know where you're going and keep your eyes on the road. Getting to heaven is like that, too. The Bible tells us, "heaven can be entered only through the narrow gate! The highway to hell is broad, and its gate is wide enough for all the multitudes who choose its easy way. But the Gateway to Life is small, and the road is narrow, and only a few ever find it" (Matthew 7:13-14). When you're traveling in an unfamiliar place, it takes concentration to stay on the right road. Are you watching your way to heaven as carefully? If not, ask God to be the navigator for your soul, and he will show you the way.

---

## 48
# How does laundry get wet when it's dry-cleaned?

Even though it's called dry cleaning, your clothes are actually getting wet. The liquid isn't water, though; it's a fast-drying chemical called perchloroethylene ("perk" for short), a combination of carbon and chlorine. Your clothes are put in a machine that pumps more than 2,000 gallons of perk and detergent per hour. A new spray of perk shoots stains away once a minute.

If this process doesn't get rid of a stain, your garment is re-treated after the dry cleaner analyzes the stain. He can use several techniques: dissolve the stain with something like a paint remover or spray it with a steam gun and blow it dry. An oxidizing bleach can take the color out of a stain, or the stain can be treated with enzymes. If you can remember to tell the dry cleaner what caused the stain, he will be able to pick the most effective way to remove it. Incidentally, dry cleaning was discovered by accident in 1855. J. B. Jolly opened the first laundry after he mistakenly spilled some turpentine on a dress and found that it was cleaned rather than stained.

Clean clothes are refreshing. Nothing, however, can compare to having a clean, clear conscience by being for-given of your sins. No dry cleaner offers that kind of ser-vice. But there's an effective procedure for treating sins yourself, and it works every time. First, you have to ana-lyze the stain—what have you done to offend God? Apolo-gize to him for those things. The stain will be gone; God removes it with his forgiveness. To protect your con-science from further soiling, apply these words from the Bible: "Turn from all known sin and spend your time in doing good. Try to live in peace with everyone; work hard at it" (Psalm 34:14).

# How did a brilliant man's name develop into "dunce"?

We use the word *dunce* to mean someone who is ignorant, and we picture a child sitting in a corner of the schoolroom with a tall triangular hat on his head. The word *dunce* actually refers to one of the most brilliant scholars of the Middle Ages. His name was John Duns Scotus, and he wrote about logic, theology, metaphysics, and grammar. He attended Oxford University, Cambridge University, and the University of Paris. How did such an educated man become associated with stupidity? It was a matter of politics.

The king of France and the pope had a disagreement over taxes. John Duns Scotus supported the pope and was banished from France. Two centuries later leaders were still angry with Scotus. They attacked his writings and his decision to side with the pope. They said that anyone who believed in John Duns Scotus was a "Duns man," which shortened to "dunce."

Many people throughout history have been persecuted for their beliefs. Those with strong opinions are most likely to be punished, perhaps because they are the easiest to identify. If you follow Jesus, you should expect the same kind of treatment and trials. Why put yourself through the humiliation?

The Bible has an answer. It says: "Don't be bewildered or surprised when you go through the fiery trials ahead, for this is no strange, unusual thing that is going to happen to you. Instead, be really glad—because these trials will make you partners with Christ in his suffering, and afterwards you will have the wonderful joy of sharing his glory in that coming day when it will be displayed. Be happy if you are cursed and insulted for being a Christian, for when that happens the Spirit of God will come upon you with great glory" (1 Peter 4:12-14). If you're going to stand strong for something, doesn't it make sense to stand for a cause that will bring you eternal rewards?

## 50

# Why did the Dutch build a memorial for a fictional character?

Have you ever heard about the little Dutch boy who put his finger in the dike to keep the ocean from flooding his city? The storybook figure was created in 1865 by Mary Maples Dodge as she told the story of Hans Brinker in her book *Silver Skates.*

Americans believed the tale. They began touring the Netherlands, asking to see the dam where the story occurred. The Dutch got tired of telling the tourists that the story was fictitious and having no one really believe them. Finally, in 1950, the Dutch gave in and built a statue showing the little

Dutch boy stopping the water with his finger. The Americans were happy with the memorial, and the Dutch were happy to collect the tourists' dollars.

The inquisitive Americans who traveled to Holland expected to find proof that the story of the Dutch boy was true. When they didn't see any, they asked someone to point the way. In this case, even with "proof," tourists didn't find truth. That's not how it is with God. He provided his "proof" for us up front. The Bible says, "The Lord himself shall give you a sign; Behold, a virgin shall conceive, and bear a son" (Isaiah 7:14, KJV). Jesus and the Bible will never prove false or fictitious. You should never feel foolish for having faith that God's Word is true. God's Word is the only absolutely permanent truth that exists on earth.

# ————————————— 51
# Why isn't the bald eagle bald?

It's common knowledge that birds have feathers. So why were we told as young children in grade school that our national emblem was the *bald* eagle? Up close, the bald eagle has dark brown feathers on its body and white feathers on its head and tail. Long ago the word *balded* in Middle English meant "white fur or feathers." This bird was called the "balded" eagle, meaning the one with white head feathers. Through time the word was shortened to *bald*.

The bald eagle is a majestic and interesting creature. It takes only one mate for its whole life, and the pair builds only one nest. Every year the birds add sticks to their nest, sometimes creating a home that weighs hundreds of pounds and measures almost 10 feet in diameter. The bald eagle was voted as the nation's official mascot in 1782. Many would say the eagle is a much more suitable emblem than the bird that Benjamin Franklin nominated. He thought that the best choice for an American symbol would be his favorite bird, the turkey.

No one can dispute the fact that the eagle displays majesty and power. In flight, it inspires awe and admiration. God understands the impact that the eagle can have on people who see it. That's why he refers to the eagle in his words of encouragement to us. "They that wait upon the Lord shall renew their strength. They shall mount up with wings like eagles; they shall run and not be weary; they shall walk and not faint" (Isaiah 40:31). Any time that you're feeling tired or discouraged, think of the eagle and spread your "wings." God's love will lift you up and carry you home.

## 52

# What do roofs and ears have in common?

How did the word *eavesdropping* come to mean listening to something that is not being addressed to you and probably is none of your business? Long ago, houses didn't have gutters on the roofs to direct rainwater away from the building. Instead, houses had overhanging roofs that came out far over the walls. These eaves kept the rainwater from dripping close to the house. There was a space under the eaves where a person could stand without getting wet, which was called the eavesdrop. If a person was listening at a window, he was probably standing under the eavesdrop and was therefore called an "eavesdropper."

You make choices every day about what you're going to listen to. The Bible says, "Not everyone who hears the Good News has welcomed it, for Isaiah the prophet said, 'Lord, who has believed me when I told them?' Yet faith comes from listening to this Good News—the Good News about Christ" (Romans 10:16-17).

If you've ever thought that you were tired of hearing about Jesus, think about this. Would you get tired of listening to someone tell you how handsome, beautiful, rich, kind, charming, or popular you are? God sees all your good qualities and possibilities. In his eyes, you are such a special person that he let his much-loved Son die for you. You are so unique and valuable to God that he wants you to be in heaven with him. No one will ever love you as much as God does. Trust in him and listen to the Good News—every word you'll hear is true.

## 53

# Where did Thomas Edison go on vacation?

Thomas Edison, inventor of the electric light and many other innovations, was well known for his intense concentration on work. At the age of 12, he was hired as a train boy to sell city newspapers and candy to railroad customers. He outsold all the other boys and proceeded to write and sell copies of his own newspaper. During the same time, he even set up a small laboratory in the back of a baggage car. The young Edison spilled some chemicals that caused a fire, and he lost his job.

As an adult, he often had trouble understanding that not everyone shared his fervor for work. Once, Edison noticed that his workers were constantly checking the factory clock during business hours. This creative employer came up with a unique way to curb the clock-watching that didn't even involve intimidation. Edison installed many clocks throughout the plant and made sure that they each showed a different time. The employees were so confused that they gave up trying to figure out the correct time and turned their attention back to work.

Edison's dedication also appeared at home. One time his wife urged him to take a much-needed vacation, but he replied that he wouldn't know where to go. She then told him to pick the one place where he'd rather be than anywhere else on earth. He agreed and said, "I'll go tomorrow."

Edison kept his word, and the next morning he went directly to his laboratory.

No one can deny that Thomas Edison had a passion for his work. He was talented, and he couldn't wait to use his abilities every day. The Bible says, "Be sure to use the abilities God has given you" (1 Timothy 4:14). If you feel drawn toward a certain field, God may be trying to guide you—but it doesn't necessarily have to be toward a career.

Perhaps you've wanted to try a new craft or to do some volunteer work because you enjoy being around other people. Maybe your talent is encouraging coworkers or writing songs or organizing things. Ask God to make clear to you what your talent is and how you can use it for him. He will either show you things about yourself that you haven't yet discovered or reinforce the direction of the journey that you have already begun.

## 54
# When was the United States ruled by an emperor?

Traditionally, an emperor is thought to have wealth, power, and prestige. Joshua Norton had none of those characteristics. Norton moved from England to San Francisco to make his fortune. He did become wealthy but lost all his money within 10 years. He ended up living in a small rooming house and working in a rice factory.

Norton thought that the United States was not being run correctly. He was a charming and gentle man, who told lots of people about his views on how to make America a better place. One newspaper editor decided to print the story, along with Norton's idea about making himself emperor of the United States.

In 1859 Norton became the self-proclaimed emperor of the United States. He wore a secondhand military uniform and a hat with a feather in it. Norton walked around San Francisco each day with his two dogs, checking on his "empire." He watched to make sure that gutters didn't have trash in them and that the streetcars kept to their schedules. If Norton saw something that he didn't like, he would "abolish" it—as he once threatened to do to Congress. When asked nicely, however, Emperor Norton would change his mind. Merchants kindly accepted his own currency, which he was allowed to print; theaters saved a special seat for him; and he ate in restaurants for free.

The people of San Francisco were delighted with their emperor. They bowed when they saw him on the street, and many citizens contributed toward his living expenses without Norton's knowledge. After 20 years of being emperor, Norton died. But he didn't have a lonely, poor man's funeral. For two entire days more than 10,000 of Norton's "subjects" paid their respects to their lovable "leader."

It's very hard to lose a job or to realize that your fortune is gone. Norton couldn't really accept it, so he invented a way that he could still make the world hold him in esteem. Make-believe answers don't usually work in the real world. If you no longer have money or power, you may wonder what's left. God loves those who can accept setbacks with grace and who continue to have faith in him. He says, "I live in that high and holy place where those with contrite, humble spirits dwell; and I refresh the humble and give new courage to those with repentant hearts" (Isaiah 57:15). God doesn't measure your importance by the balance in your bank account. Let him show you how to search for "riches" within yourself.

# 55
# How did some prisoners dig themselves into deeper trouble?

A group of prisoners in Mexico was planning a daring, underground escape. They carefully calculated how far it would be to dig past the prison walls and secretly began working on a tunnel. After several months the passageway was complete, and the time to escape arrived. Seventy-five convicts traveled underground, through the tunnel, and beyond the prison boundaries. Everything went according to plan until the very last minute. As the escapees emerged, they realized that they had dug their tunnel directly into a courtroom.

It's a good guess that the prisoners wouldn't have gotten away with their escape, although justice was extremely swift in their case. We expect that people who do wrong intentionally will bring bad things on themselves. That's one of the messages of the Bible. It says, "Do not those who plot evil go astray? But those who plan what is good find love and faithfulness" (Proverbs 14:22, NIV). The best way to avoid trouble is to dig into God's Word and steer clear of evil.

## 56
# Why does one eye work harder than the other?

Did you know that you have a dominant eye? Your brain chooses this eye to receive its visual impressions when both of your eyes are open. You can do a simple test to find out which of your eyes is the dominant one.

Hold a pencil up with your arm outstretched in front of you. With both eyes open, line the pencil up to a straight line in the distance—the edge of a wall, door, picture frame, or the trunk of a tree (any straight line will do). Now close one eye at a time. When you're looking through one eye, the pencil will appear to stay exactly where you lined it up, even with the edge you've chosen. But when you close that eye and open the other, you'll discover that the pencil appears to have moved—even jumped—to one side or the other. It will no longer look lined up to the edge. How do you interpret this? The eye that made the pencil appear to stay even with the edge is your dominant eye. That's the one your brain is using to record what you're seeing.

God wants you to understand the power of your eyes. It's a much bigger issue than simply having an acuity of $^{20}/_{20}$. The Bible tells us, "If your eye is pure, there will be sunshine in your soul. But if your eye is clouded with evil thoughts and desires, you are in deep spiritual darkness. And oh, how deep that darkness can be!" (Matthew 6:22-23). If life seems blurry, confusing, or distorted, adjust your soul by focusing on Jesus, and let the Son shine in!

---

## 57
# Why doesn't a fan cool the air?

On a hot day the idea of cooling off in front of an electric fan sounds appealing. We sit very close and count on the fan to make us more comfortable by lowering the air temperature. But that's not really what happens. A fan can actually make a room hotter because of the warmth from the running motor. Fans don't cool the temperature of the air at all—they just blow the same hot air around. So why does a fan make us feel better?

The fan moves air against our skin, which causes perspiration to evaporate. If we couldn't sweat, our body temperature would rise so high that we would die. We have sweat glands all over our body, but the largest ones are in our palms, forehead, armpits, and the soles of our feet. We notice our perspiration the most in those places. Even though the air temperature doesn't get cooler when a fan is blowing, we feel cooler as evaporation occurs and our body temperature drops.

In the same way that you can look forward to your body feeling better in front of a fan, you can look forward to refreshment for your spirit in the presence of God. If you dream of having some "cooling-off time" from your hectic schedule, ask God to blow the revitalizing breath of his calmness into your soul. The Bible tells us, "He quiets the raging oceans and all the world's clamor" (Psalm 65:7). Spend a few minutes in God's peace, being comforted by the absence of chaos. You'll be revived and ready to begin again.

## 58

# When did paying a library fine make history?

In 1823 a man borrowed a book from the medical library at the University of Cincinnati. Nothing was unusual about that—until later. Much later. One hundred and forty years later, to be exact, when the borrower's great-grandson, Richard Dodd, walked into the library and returned the book for his late great-grandfather. The fine, which was in excess of $2,000, was waived, but as far as anyone knows, it still stands as the fine for the longest-overdue book.

Richard did an unusual thing by caring enough to try to

resolve his relative's debt. There are quite a few people who probably try to avoid paying their own debts, much less someone else's. If we knew of someone who was willing to pay the debts of everyone on earth, we would be shocked because it would be too much generosity to comprehend. But that's exactly what Jesus did when he died on the cross for us.

He said, "I must be lifted up upon a pole, so that anyone who believes in me will have eternal life. For God loved the world so much that he gave his only Son so that anyone who believes in him shall not perish but have eternal life. God did not send his Son into the world to condemn it, but to save it" (John 3:14-17). Mankind's sins were too great—we could never repay God for them. But Jesus released us from our debt by dying on our behalf, making it possible for us to go to heaven. The Bible tells about God's love for us and is one book that will never be overdue.

---

## 59
# What plant only grows after being burned by a fire?

A forest fire usually destroys all the plants and trees in its path and prevents regrowth in that area for a while. In South Africa, however, the protea can only grow if there *is* a fire. The head of this strange national flower contains the seeds and can stay tightly sealed in a hard shell for almost 20 years. The shell doesn't open until it's scorched again and the fire is over. The light, fluffy seeds are then blown to the ground by the wind, where they begin to grow.

As Christians, the Bible tells us, "When you walk through the fire, you will not be burned; the flames will not set you ablaze" (Isaiah 43:2, NIV). This doesn't mean that Christian people have different bodies. What the Bible means is that if you believe in Jesus Christ, the devil cannot take your soul, no matter how hard he tries to lead you away from God. You will be able to walk through all the devil's tricks by holding on to Jesus, and your soul will not be singed.

## 60 How did the meaning of a flag at half-mast change?

When the American flag flies at half-mast, we know that someone important to our country has died. The custom started on ships as far back as the 1600s. When a ship was forced to surrender, it flew its flag at half-mast as proof that it was acknowledging its enemy's superiority. It was a sign that room was being made to put the victor's flag at the top of the pole.

After the conquered ship reached shore, the flag stayed at half-mast as a gesture of honor and respect to the sailors who had died trying to defend the ship. Any other type of death on board also was signaled by the half-mast flag. By the 1700s, the tradition was being copied on land. The flag at half-mast first was a sign of defeat but later became a sign of honor.

The cross on which Jesus was crucified had the same change of meaning. When Jesus died on the cross, it was only human to assume that he had been defeated. For three days the cross stood as a reminder to everyone that those who had followed Christ had apparently been betrayed. People thought that the disciples should surrender their beliefs and admit that they had been wrong. Then came the turnaround.

Jesus Christ rose again. Not only did he come back to life, but he let his followers know that they, too, could have a fresh chance. The Bible says, "Your old sin-loving nature was buried with him by baptism when he died; and when God the Father, with glorious power, brought him back to life again, you were given his wonderful new life to enjoy" (Romans 6:4). The cross became a symbol of honor. Christ had kept his word. He was truly the Son of God, and his promises of a new life for us were verified beyond doubt. The cross serves as a symbol honoring Christ's death, just as the half-mast flag honors the death of a beloved citizen.

## 61

# Why aren't there any fleas at a flea market?

Flea markets are groups of booths, usually out-doors, that sell a variety of goods at discount prices. Where did the name come from? You might think that it refers to seedy, flea-bitten merchandise. But the word *flea* isn't a description—it's a mispronunciation.

It started in New York at one of the first outdoor markets called the Vallie Market. A sign was made to help people find the location, but it turned out to be too small for the whole name to fit. The name was written as "Vle. Market." People started calling it the "vlee" market because that's what the abbreviation looked like. This was repeated until it sounded like *flea*. Now every open-air market is referred to by this strange label.

It's funny how even our most inconsequential actions can have such a big impact. The person who made the flea market sign probably never even thought twice about what he had written. He had no idea that years later people would refer to the abbreviation on his simple sign. You never know what little thing will turn out to be important. That's why the Bible tells us, "Be a good workman, one who does not need to be ashamed when God examines your work" (2 Timothy 2:15). By keeping your eyes on the details, you will have the assurance that you did your best and created a lasting impression.

# Are you seeing things?

Who are those annoying little dots and threads that drift around in your eyesight? You try blinking, rolling your eyes, and looking somewhere else, but they don't disappear. They're known by a name that truly describes them—"floaters"—and you're stuck with them for life.

How did they get inside your eyes? Blood was carried to your eye by the hyaloid artery while you were in the womb. When your eye finished developing, this artery shriveled up and disintegrated into pieces that were then permanently caught in your vision. Floaters can also increase with age. Tiny veins on the retina can rupture or leak, causing more blood to drift through the vitreous humor, the transparent jellylike fluid that fills the eyeball behind the lens.

The Bible has an interesting observation about irritating things in the eyes. Even though floaters can't be removed, we'd take them out if we could because they're occasionally bothersome. We tend to also be bothered by faults we see in someone else, and this is why the Bible cautions us: "Do not judge, or you too will be judged. For in the same way you judge others, you will be judged, and with the measure you use, it will be measured to you. Why do you look at the speck of sawdust in your brother's eye and pay no attention to the plank in your own eye? How can you say to your brother, 'Let me take the speck out of your eye,' when all the time there is a plank in your own eye? You hypocrite, first take the plank out of your own eye, and then you will see clearly to remove the speck from your brother's eye" (Matthew 7:1-5, NIV).

# 63
# Which flower looks like a lion's teeth?

Two common flowers got their names from the way they look. The dandelion is technically a weed that flowers into a white feathery ball. In French, its fluffy seeds were described as *dent de lion*, which translated to "teeth of the lion." Dandelions weren't eaten by lions, but some people used to put them in salads. Another flower with an interesting name is the daisy. Daisies open up in the morning, showing their bright yellow centers. In the evening, they close. That's why the English called it the "daeg-eseage," which meant "day's eye."

It's easy to see why daisies would seem to be opening their eyes in the morning. God knows that we enjoy the light of day after the dark of night. The Bible tells us how we can keep spiritual light with us all the time. It says, "Before you turn to God and stretch out your hands to him, get rid of your sins and leave all iniquity behind you. Only then, without the spots of sin to defile you, can you walk steadily forward to God without fear. Only then can you forget your misery. It will all be in the past. And your life will be cloudless; any darkness will be as bright as morning!" (Job 11:13-17). Begin your new life like the dawning of a new day!

# Who used fingerprints to make a contract binding?

Fingerprinting is not a modern idea. In Babylonia authors pressed their fingerprints into clay tablets to prove whose work it was and to prevent forgery. The Chinese put fingerprints on their official documents long ago. One man in India, however, was responsible for the first modern use of fingerprinting in 1858.

William Hershel was in the Indian civil service when he used oil ink to take the palm print, which also included the fingers, of a local contractor who had agreed to supply some metal. Hershel wasn't trying to identify the man; he just wanted to impress on the man that he couldn't back out of the contract.

Hershel then began a registry of fingerprints by taking samples from his coworkers and friends. In 1877 Hershel used fingerprints for official reasons. He wanted to keep army personnel from getting their pensions paid twice. Fingerprinting was also used to stop prisoners from hiring someone else to serve their sentences. But he didn't think of the possibilities of finding criminals. That idea came along later, after a man named Sir Francis Galton made a huge fingerprint collection. Scotland Yard was impressed and decided to use fingerprinting as a way to catch criminals.

To a fingerprint expert, your hands can identify you. To others, your hands can also reveal who you really are. Most of us say a lot about ourselves by what we do with our hands. The Bible says, "The character of even a child can be known by the way he acts—whether what he does is pure and right" (Proverbs 20:11). If a little boy throws rocks at your dog every day on the way home from school, you form an opinion about that child based on the actions of his hands. In the same way, hands that distribute sandwiches at a homeless shelter "say" something different than hands that burglarize cars. Let your hands identify you as someone who works for God.

## 65

# Why did W. C. Fields open so many bank accounts?

The actor W. C. Fields was not always the dapper, wealthy, wry man that he appeared to be in the movies. He had many hard times when he was young, knowing first-hand about poverty and hunger. Because of this, he had an unusually intense fear of being broke. The comedian often had nightmares about being penniless, alone, and chased by the police in a strange city.

Fields came up with a plan to comfort himself. In every new city he opened a bank account under a false name and deposited whatever money he had with him at the time. Sometimes it was a few coins, sometimes it was $50,000. Fields probably felt more secure knowing that he could withdraw his money from most any bank. He once told a friend that he had opened more than 700 accounts. Unfortunately, Fields kept such poor records that only 23 accounts could be traced after his death in 1946. It is estimated that $1.3 millon of his money was never found.

It didn't do Fields much good to spend his life accumulating money and storing it away. He was putting his faith in his possessions, expecting them to bring him security and peace. But Fields's nightmares kept occurring because his trust was misplaced.

The Bible says, "When you lie down, you will not be afraid; when you lie down, your sleep will be sweet. Have no fear of sudden disaster or of the ruin that overtakes the wicked, for the Lord will be your confidence and will keep your foot from being snared" (Proverbs 3:24-26, NIV). The only true way to feel safe is to put your trust in God. He can, and will, take care of you much better than you could ever take care of yourself.

---

# 66
# What is the five-year frog?

A very strange frog lives in central Australia. It's called the water-holding frog, and it has been equipped for survival with some unique capabilities. Rain, which rarely comes to the frog's desert home, is the biggest event in its life.

The frog climbs out of its underground home as the rain begins. The first thing it does is to absorb the water through its specially designed skin, which causes the frog to blow up like a balloon. Next, it eats a tremendous quantity of insects. Eggs are then laid in the puddles, and the next generation begins. The tadpoles develop the ability to breathe air in just a few weeks—much faster than other frogs since the pools where they swim evaporate quickly.

When all the rainwater has dried up, the adult and young frogs dig underground to make a small living space. They move in and then make an "envelope" from skin secretions that cover their bodies. The membrane helps their bodies retain the moisture they've collected. It even has an airhole for breathing. The frogs become still and don't move for up to five or six years, when the next rainfall comes and the whole process begins again.

Not too many people are aware that a creature like this even exists. We certainly haven't been personally concerned about its ability to survive. Yet God created this frog to take care of itself. When we begin to inspect the world around us, we find unlimited ways that God is running the universe very efficiently without our input. Grass grows, a cloud blows, water flows. The list is endless. But what does this mean to you?

The Bible gives a suggestion: "Look at the birds! They don't worry about what to eat—they don't need to sow or reap or store up food—for your heavenly Father feeds them. And you are far more valuable to him than they are" (Matthew 6:26). Your survival is important to God because he loves you and wants to take care of you. So the next time you doubt whether God can fix your problem and you try to handle it yourself—stop. Count the birds, the trees, the blades of grass. Try to make the wind blow or the rain fall. You will be reminded of who's in charge—and why.

## 67
# Why was the general always absent during roll call?

During World War II, General Douglas MacArthur meant a great deal to the people of the Philippines. When the general was recalled from the Philippine Islands in 1942, he made his famous promise, "I shall return."

General MacArthur kept his word and came back two years later to liberate the Philippines from the Japanese. In gratitude, the Congress of the Philippines honored General MacArthur by promising to call out his name from that day forward at every parade roll call of the Philippine army. When the general's name was spoken, a senior officer would answer, "Present in spirit."

This gesture touched General MacArthur deeply. He cried when he heard of the plan, something he hadn't done since he was a boy. General MacArthur visited the Philippine Islands one more time at age 81, and true to their word, the citizens called out his name during roll call as they had been doing for the last 36 years. The people of the Philippine Islands were as faithful to General MacArthur as he had been to them. Once again the general cried.

It was very meaningful to General MacArthur to be remembered that way. Sometimes we wonder if God has forgotten us. It seems as if we're all alone, and we wonder if we've been abandoned. But you have God's promise that he will not leave you. His assurances are found time and time again in the Bible. The next time you are doubting God's interest in you, remember what he has said: "I will not forget you! See, I have engraved you on the palms of my hands" (Isaiah 49:15-16, NIV). He will return for you—that's a promise!

# 68

# When did spaghetti grow on trees?

Did you know that spaghetti noodles don't grow on trees? Apparently lots of people weren't aware of this fact, and they proved it on April Fools' Day 1957. An English current-events television program called *Panorama* chose to run an unusual news story on April 1, the traditional day for playing pranks.

Viewers watched pictures of women picking long noodles off the limbs of trees and drying the spaghetti in the sun. The narrator was a much trusted broadcaster, who calmly told about the annual spaghetti harvest taking place on the border of Switzerland and Italy. He ended his report by commenting on the goodness of homegrown spaghetti. Some people thought a joke shouldn't be played on a serious news show. Others thought the joke was funny. But many viewers sent in requests to the television show, wanting to know how they could attend the spaghetti harvest themselves next year.

Sometimes it's hard to tell what's really true. Although the spaghetti harvest was a harmless joke, people can be deceptive, cunning, and persuasive on purpose. But Jesus is never any of those things. He says, "If you hold to my teaching, you are really my disciples. Then you will know the truth, and the truth will set you free" (John 8:31-32, NIV). When you love Jesus, you don't need to fear what others might say or do. He will help you weed out the right information from the wrong.

---

## 69
# What did gloves say about hands?

You can probably think of someone you know who "talks with her hands," making many gestures and movements to accentuate her thoughts. But you may not know that throughout history, people have used gloves to "speak" for them.

It began with gloves telling that the wearer was part of royalty. These gloves, as you might expect, were embellished with precious stones, jewels, and gold embroidery. Royal gloves were sometimes given to others as a show of support. On market days in Germany, the king's glove was placed in a public spot to warn thieves not to attempt a robbery. A lady would give her glove to a favorite knight as a token of her affection, and the knight would carry it with him into battle. At a king's coronation, a glove was always tossed to the ground as a challenge to anyone who wanted to capture the crown. This was known as "throwing down the gauntlet."

By the sixteenth century, gloves were perfumed in the belief that the smell would keep diseases away. That proved to be a false notion, but people still enjoyed the scent because bathing was rare. People showed concern for beauty, softening their hands at night by wearing gloves made out of chicken skin. In many portraits, however, the subjects are only holding their gloves or wearing just one. What do those gloves tell us? That they weren't made very skillfully and probably didn't fit their owner. Queen Elizabeth I once had such a pair, with thumbs that measured over five inches long.

Gloves were used in history as protection for reputation, beauty, or power. But when we're feeling lonely, afraid, and threatened, a glove is no help at all. We need the armor of God. The Bible tells us about this armor. It says: "Stand firm then, with the belt of truth buckled around your waist, with the breastplate of righteousness in place, and with your feet fitted with the readiness that comes from the gospel of peace. In addition to all this, take up the shield of faith, with which you can extinguish all the flaming arrows of the evil one. Take the helmet of salvation and the sword of the Spirit, which is the word of God" (Ephesians 6:14-17, NIV).

How do you get all this protection? It's free for the asking. Invite God to come into your life, and he will equip you with his power.

─────────────────────────────── **70**

# How did riches escape the man who started a gold rush?

One man single-handedly started one of the world's largest gold rushes. The year was 1886, and the place was South Africa. George Walker made a report about a "payable gold field" that he had discovered. When word got out, Johannesburg grew from a sleepy collection of shacks and tents to an important city. Gold diggers arrived from around the world during the next three years.

The gold vein was 50 miles long and served as the world's leading gold source for the next 30 years. Later, even more land was discovered to contain gold—more than 300 miles and 800 tons of gold. Walker should have been unbelievably rich since he started the whole search, but for reasons unknown, he sold out too soon. In exchange for his claim of the Witwatersrand (which means "ridge of white waters") gold deposits, Walker received less than $50.

Walker gave up too soon and missed out on a great reward. He obviously couldn't see far enough ahead to be reassured that if he stayed firm, he would receive a prize far beyond his biggest dreams. God tells us that believing in Jesus and staying committed to him will bring us the reward of heaven, which is so spectacular we can't begin to imagine it. We don't have to wonder what might be ahead or make a judgment call without the benefit of facts. The Bible encourages us when it says, "Let us not get tired of doing what is right, for after a while we will reap a harvest of blessing if we don't get discouraged and give up" (Galatians 6:9). Stake your claim on Jesus because he promises us true blessings.

## 71
# Why don't we eat goldfish?

Many years ago the Chinese figured out that raising their own fish for food would be an economical idea. They needed a fish that was hardy and could live well in shallow water with little oxygen. The best candidate was the goldfish, at the time a greenish bronze member of the carp family.

As the Chinese cultivated and bred the fish, its color changed to gold. People began to admire the goldfish for its looks and became interested in keeping the fish as decorations for their gardens. Once the wealthy had their garden ponds stocked with goldfish, the fish became a fad. Europeans also wanted goldfish as pets, and the Chinese found that there was more money in raising the fish for their beautiful color than for their taste. Hatcheries developed quickly, and in just a short time there were more than 100 varieties of goldfish—but not enough buyers. Children are still fascinated by this fish that is now considered ordinary, but think twice before supplying your youngster with a bowlful. Goldfish have been known to live for more than 14 years!

People have always admired things of beauty. Imagine their delight when they first saw the shiny, wriggling, sparkling goldfish! Yet, eventually the glamour and appeal of the special fish tarnished. Nothing on earth is meant to last forever. The Bible tells us what should be important to us as Christians. It says, "Good sense is far more valuable than gold or precious jewels" (Proverbs 20:15). Don't be distracted by glitz and glitter—it might be fool's gold. Concentrate on learning all you can from God's Word, because that's what gives you wisdom and makes you rich in spirit.

## 72

# How did golf courses end up with 18 holes?

Most golf courses are made up of 18 holes. But that's not how early courses were designed. Originally, each course had a different number of holes to play. The number of holes at each location depended on how much land was available to build the course.

The first golf course, Saint Andrews in Scotland, only had 11 holes. But the golfers played each hole twice, so a game at Saint Andrews was 22-holes long. After a while, course designers made some holes harder by making them longer. Other holes were left out, and by 1764 a total round was set at 18 holes.

Perhaps the strangest golf courses, along with the most unusual jobs, were created during World War II. The United States was concerned for the security of its airplane-manufacturing plants. Grass was grown on the roofs to create the illusion—from the air—that pilots were seeing only golf courses. And the odd jobs? People were hired to play on these courses to complete the creative scenery.

One of the goals of every golfer is to avoid the sand traps that engulf the ball and make playing harder. Life has pitfalls, and the consequences of falling into them are much more serious than in a golf game. The Bible tells us that a man who rejects God will have problems: "The vigor of his step is weakened; his own schemes throw him down. His feet thrust him into a net and he wanders into its mesh. A trap seizes him by the heel; a snare holds him fast. A noose is hidden for him on the ground; a trap lies in his path" (Job 18:7-10, NIV). Are you practicing your strategy for life as carefully as you're practicing your golf game? Ask God to guide you through life's course, and you will avoid getting trapped.

# How did a fruit foul up a publicity stunt?

It seemed like a good idea at the time. In 1915 Wilbert Robinson, manager of the Brooklyn Dodgers, agreed to do a publicity stunt. The plan was for an airplane to fly overhead and drop a baseball to Wilbert, who would try to catch it.

The pilot was Ruth Law, a famous aviator. She was supposed to receive a baseball at the airport from someone on the team, but no one had arrived to deliver the ball by take-off time. The plane's mechanic offered Ruth a nearby substitute, which she took on the flight and consequently dropped as planned.

Down below, Wilbert was waiting, but he missed the round object. Instead, it hit him on the head. Wilbert began screaming that he was dead—he had stinging, blinding liquid dripping into his eyes, and big hard chunks of something were falling from his head. He panicked, thinking that blood was flowing from his skull, which had just cracked into pieces. It took a few minutes for Wilbert to realize what the mechanic had given Ruth to drop from her plane instead of the baseball. Wilbert had just been hit by a large grapefruit.

When Wilbert was hit on the head with the grapefruit, the first reaction of the crowd in the stadium was probably to laugh. We are, after all, human. But this wasn't funny to the baseball manager. As the spectators were being amused, he was experiencing terror. The Bible reminds us to consider the other guy's feelings. It says, "When others are happy, be happy with them. If they are sad, share their sorrow" (Romans 12:15). It's not our natural response, but we can learn to do it. When you have compassion for your fellow-man, you are showing how God has taught you compassion by his example.

## 74

# What causes gray hair?

As you get older, gray is not a color that's added to your hair—it's color that's subtracted. When you're young, your body manufactures pigment, or color, that enters each of your hair shafts through the follicles in your scalp. This pigment, called melanin, supplies your hair with its natural color. As you age, melanin production slows down, and the hair shafts become more clear than colored. Less color means the appearance of more white or gray hair when light strikes it.

Getting gray hair takes a while because hair only grows about a half-inch each month. If it seems to you that someone's hair "turned gray overnight," you've probably witnessed a case of an inflamed scalp. The gray hairs are most resistant, so they will stay in the scalp. The darker hairs fall out more quickly, so what's left suddenly looks grayer or whiter than before.

There's another way of looking at your gray hair. The

world might tell you that it means you're getting old and washed out, but the Bible tells another story. It says, "White hair is a crown of glory and is seen most among the godly" (Proverbs 16:31). Cherish your silver tresses. You aren't obligated to dye your hair. In fact, if you do, you may be covering up one of your most valuable assets!

---

## 75
# Why are two security guards hired to stare up all day?

At the John Hancock Tower in Boston, two full-time guards spend all their time staring straight up through their binoculars. What are they looking at? Their job is to report any cracks or discolorations in the more than 10,000 windows throughout the 60-story building. Such diligence is necessary. The Hancock Tower has a historic problem with panes.

The building was started in 1968 and completed four years later. It still couldn't be used for another four years because of a mysterious problem. The windows kept popping out by the dozens—large 4-by-11-foot panes that shattered to the ground. Once, all the windows were replaced with huge 400-pound sections of thick tempered glass. But the new windows popped out, also. When Boston was hit by 75-mile-per-hour winds, 65 windows exploded and hundreds more were damaged as the glass flew.

When one quarter of the windows were boarded up as architects tried to decide what to do, the Tower was nick-named the "Plywood Palace." It was determined that the sway of the building was putting too much stress on the windows, so gigantic weights were used to anchor the building from inside. Even though this improved the problem, guards remain posted as an extra safeguard.

Maybe sometimes you feel a little like the John Hancock Tower. You have so many stresses and are being pulled in so many different directions that you are having trouble keeping all the pieces of your life together. God doesn't want you to live this way. He knows that you can't enjoy life when you're constantly harried. He wants more for you. Maybe you can't change the circumstances around you, but you can get relief.

You can begin relying on the fact that "God is our refuge and strength, an ever-present help in trouble. Therefore we will not fear, though the earth give way and the mountains fall into the heart of the sea, though its waters roar and foam and the mountains quake with their surging" (Psalm 46:1-3, NIV). God will bear your burdens for you if you let him. Don't be afraid to ask him, because once you have, you won't need to feel fragile during life's strong winds.

# What are some predictable differences in people's hands?

Although there are exceptions to every rule, there are some interesting comparisons between the male and female hand. If you watch people's hands carefully, you may notice for yourself that these "rules" are often true. Test them!

1. A man's ring finger is longer than his index finger, or pointer. A woman's pointer is longer than her ring finger.
2. If you ask people to show you their hands, a man puts his hands out with the palms up. A woman turns hers palms down.
3. If a man is looking at his fingernails, his hand is usually turned up with his fingers curled. A woman turns her palms down and her fingers straight.
4. On both men's and women's hands, their middle finger is almost always exactly as long as their palm is wide.

What we humans do with our hands is nothing compared to what God does with his. The Bible praises God's handiwork when it says, "In the beginning you laid the foundations of the earth, and the heavens are the work of your hands" (Psalm 102:25, NIV).

If someone told you that you had to copy the world that God made, how would you do it? How could you make a star? or a mountain? How would you make a flower open up or give a dog its bark or get a cloud to hang in the sky? What would you do to get a river to flow? God knows how to create all of these things and how to keep them working. Our job is to enjoy them and to thank God for giving us such a wonderful world.

## 77
# When was Hollywood a happy little hamlet?

Did you know that Hollywood was intended to be a model community for nondrinkers in its beginning? It was founded by the Wilcox family, who bought the land in 1887. The name *Hollywood* was picked by Mrs. Wilcox. She had been seated on a train next to a woman who had a summer home by that name and liked the sound of it. Imagine a community with no crime, not even a jail, and where the mayor worked as a volunteer. For 20 years Hollywood was a hamlet of 500 residents with no bigger problems than how to keep sheep away from the town square.

Ten years later Hollywood turned into the nation's movie capital for two reasons. First, the weather made a longer filming season possible. Second, movie executives were often worried about being prosecuted for infringing on patents. Hollywood was close enough to Mexico that they could cross the border for immunity if necessary.

Films were first called "movies" by the people of Hollywood because filming required such constant movement and activity. The "Hollywood" sign started out as "Hollywoodland," an advertising gimmick for a realty firm. The last four letters fell off, and "Hollywood" was left on the hillside.

Many aspiring actors and actresses flock to Hollywood in hopes of gaining fame and fortune. To some, becoming well known must seem like the ultimate success. But the Bible advises us to strive for something more valuable. It says, "But where can wisdom be found? Where does understanding dwell? Man does not comprehend its worth; it cannot be found in the land of the living" (Job 28:12-13, NIV). Don't spend your time searching for spotlights to bring you happiness or wealth—search the Scriptures instead.

# 78
# Why doesn't humble pie taste good?

When we are forced to admit that we are wrong about something, we often describe it by saying that we had to "eat humble pie." What we really mean is that we were made to feel less proud of ourselves. But this is not what the phrase was intended to say. The word we normally use for *humble* comes from the Latin word for *earth,* which is *humus.* We tend to think of someone humble as "down to earth," or not having many pretensions.

But the phrase "eating humble pie" comes from a very different history. It doesn't have anything to do with the word *humble* as we know it today. Long ago, people who were poor had to eat some undesirable parts of animals in their pies because they couldn't afford the better meats. Their pies often contained such ingredients as the umbilical cords of animals. The rich would have nothing to do with this "umble" (as in "umbilical cord") pie. If you were forced to eat "umble pie," it didn't mean that you had a meek personality. It meant that you had a lack of funds.

Maybe you can identify with the people who had to eat umble pie. When you're threatened and troubled by money problems, it might be time to stop and ask yourself why you are so worried. You will probably come up with the idea that in today's world, money means security. But God has some words of wisdom for you that may make a difference in your priorities.

He says, "Do not store up riches for yourselves here on earth, where moths and rust destroy, and robbers break in and steal. Instead, store up riches for yourselves in heaven, where moths and rust cannot destroy, and robbers cannot break in and steal. For your heart will always be where your riches are" (Matthew 6:19-21, TEV). God wants you to know that your heart is immeasurably more valuable than what's in your wallet. Who you are does not depend on what you own. Concentrate on multiplying your faith, and God will work on multiplying your blessings.

# Which artist always depicted children but never had any?

When Berta Hummel was young, her family didn't have very much paper, so she practiced her favorite activity, drawing, on the margins of letters and papers from the trash. Her father never fulfilled his desire to become an artist because he needed to work in the family business. To make sure that his daughter got her chance, Berta was sent to the Munich Academy of Applied Arts, where she excelled. Berta became a nun with the chosen name of Maria Innocentia and kept drawing pictures of children that everyone enjoyed. Her drawings were put on postcards and eventually turned into ceramic figurines by Franz Goebel.

The figurines are prized for their workmanship. With as many as 39 individual parts, the ceramic figurines were hollow so they wouldn't burst in the firing ovens. In addition, each figurine went through a series of 25 checks to assure its quality. In 1952 the United States Treasury declared the hobby of collecting M. I. Hummel figurines an "American pastime." Sister Maria Innocentia never knew of her work's immense popularity, though. She died of tuberculosis in 1946 when she was 37.

The figurines of M. I. Hummel are truly a celebration of

childhood. God encourages us to treat children with extra care. They are very special to him. He tells us, "Beware that you don't look down upon a single one of these little children. For I tell you that in heaven their angels have constant access to my Father" (Matthew 18:10). It pleases God when you treat all children as the treasures they are to him.

# 80

# How can you get to sleep without counting sheep?

The clock is ticking, everyone else is asleep (at least it seems that way), and you're staring at the ceiling in the dark, getting tenser by the minute. All of us have experienced this type of sleepless night once in a while. But there are steps you can take to avoid being awake too many nights—and they don't involve counting sheep.

First, set a schedule and try to stick to it. Rise and retire at the same consistent times, even on weekends and holidays. If you're positively not sleepy, don't continue to lie in bed. Get up and do something that relaxes you, like soaking your feet in hot water for 10 minutes (which moves blood concentration from brain to feet, making your thoughts less active.) Exercise on a regular basis: The best times are mornings or late afternoons. Stay away from caffeine. Try to eliminate things that disturb you while going to sleep—like a bright light or a dripping faucet.

There's another way to get to sleep—talk to God. The Bible says, "I cried out to the Lord, and he heard me from his Temple in Jerusalem. Then I lay down and slept in peace and woke up safely, for the Lord was watching over me. And now, although ten thousand enemies surround me on every side, I am not afraid" (Psalm 3:4-6).

If you feel vulnerable or anxious, allow God to share your burdens. Ask him to take upon himself what seems overwhelming to you. It pleases God when you show your trust in him. You can rest assured, counting on the fact that he knows best how to resolve your difficulties.

---

## 81
# What do the letters *IOU* mean?

When you borrow money from someone, you might give them an informal receipt that uses the letters *IOU*, which is intended to stand for "I owe you." That's not, however, what these three letters mean. In the past, someone writing this type of receipt would print, "I owe unto . . ." and then add the name of the lender. "I owe unto" was abbreviated through time as IOU.

What comes after the IOU on your receipts? The Bible says, "Don't withhold repayment of your debts. Don't say 'some other time,' if you can pay now" (Proverbs 3:27-28). Some people rationalize their debts by telling themselves, "I need the money more than they do. They won't miss it. I can do more good with it than they would." But God doesn't want you to think that way. He doesn't want you to be dependent on anyone. He wants you to keep your word, repay the money quickly, and be free from every obligation. When you are honorable in all things, you can have respect for yourself and receive the respect of others.

## 82

# Why has ironing always been a chore?

If you're stuck with a pile of ironing, remember that it used to be worse! At first, heated iron bars were rolled across Greek clothes, and metal hammers were used to beat wrinkles out of Roman materials. Then, an upside-down-mushroom-shaped iron was rocked across damp clothes by the Vikings. Multiple pleats were a sign of Viking wealth—the poor didn't have enough time or servants to have pleats pressed into their clothes.

By the 1400s "hot box" irons were used in Europe by the wealthy. These irons were filled with a hot brick or hot coals. For the poor, a flat piece of metal with a handle was heated by returning it to the fire many times. But different designs for irons caused problems. The fire-heated irons got soot on the clothes. The gas-heated irons of the 1800s could leak or even explode. By 1882 the first electric iron was invented by Henry Weely, but it took a long time to heat up, and not many people had electricity. It wasn't until 1926 that the steam iron made its first appearance.

The worst part of ironing is that it isn't permanent. No matter how beautifully you iron out the wrinkles, after the clothes are worn, the wrinkles return. Life is like that. You try your best to straighten out the wrinkles in your life: your troubles, your fears, your weaknesses. But it seems as soon as you smooth those creases, other areas appear that need work. Don't get discouraged.

The Bible tells us, "We are pressed on every side by troubles, but not crushed and broken. We are perplexed because we don't know why things happen as they do, but we don't give up and quit. We are hunted down, but God never abandons us. We get knocked down, but we get up again and keep going" (2 Corinthians 4:8-9). Ask God to keep you perfectly pressed.

# 83

## Who listened to Mozart and Shakespeare while stranded on a desert island?

The next time you feel harried by the fast pace of life and dream of being on a deserted island, think again! It happened to Henri and Jose Bourdens in 1966, and it wasn't much fun. The Bourdens had been traveling for pleasure on their yacht from Singapore to the Celebes Islands. The wind caused them to lose pieces from their yacht. Their disabled craft soon ran out of fuel, and the food supply ran low as well.

They floated for more than a month, eating rice, flour, and sugar until they washed ashore on an island near Australia. The husband and wife were able to collect some supplies from the yacht, including a Bible, a record player that ran on batteries, a sail, some spices, and the works of Shakespeare, Mozart, and Bach. Soon afterward the yacht was destroyed against the rocks.

After a week, they still hadn't seen another person. The sail was stretched to catch rainwater, and sometimes they ate snails as a treat. The one time they ventured off to look for help, the Bourdens got caught in a swamp with mosquitoes, snakes, and crocodiles for three days. They finally were able to return to their camp, but after two months they decided no one was coming to rescue them.

They built a raft and tried to sail away from the island, but the raft began to sink slowly. Crabs nipped at their legs, and they were terrified of sharks. Just as Henri and Jose were accepting the fact that they would die on the ocean, they saw a boat. Their one remaining smoke bomb was soaked, but it lit anyway and was seen by their rescuers.

Have you ever thought that if you could just live by yourself and didn't have to deal with anyone, you'd be happy? God understands that feeling. People are messy; they're unpredictable; they're aggravating. If it weren't for people, God's children could spend all their time sharing glorious moments with him. But that's not God's plan.

The Bible says, "You are the world's light—a city on a hill, glowing in the night for all to see. Don't hide your light! Let it shine for all; let your good deeds glow for all to see, so that they will praise your heavenly Father" (Matthew 5:14-16). If you're not where people are, you can't show them what God means to you. There's nothing wrong with taking a vacation to "recharge your battery" as long as you come back ready to shine!

---

# 84
# How did the Jacuzzi get its name?

Did you know that the popular Jacuzzi has its history in airplanes and arthritis? The Italian family of Candido Jacuzzi came to America in 1917. They began manufacturing equipment for airplanes, but they left the aviation business after a monoplane they had designed crashed with fatalities. The family then invented a water-injection pump for swimming pools.

Candido was watching his young son, Kenneth, in a hospital whirlpool, which he used as treatment for rheumatoid arthritis. Candido saw that his family's pump was similar to the one in the healing bath, so he developed a home version of the whirlpool and sold it through medical stores.

Hollywood, with its health-oriented residents, started a Jacuzzi trend by installing the tubs in their homes and by later purchasing portable versions. In 1975 the Jacuzzi's business was sold for $70 million, but they will always be connected to the tubs by their name.

The Bible tells of an ill man who told Jesus, "'I have no one to help me into the pool when the water is stirred'" (John 5:7, NIV). Jesus healed this man when he saw that the man couldn't reach the water. Candido found his life's work by trying to help his son get to the water. Jesus filled the ill man's need; Candido filled his son's need. If you're looking for a way to make your life meaningful, follow these examples. Look for a need that you can help fill. In doing so, you will discover that you're helping yourself as well.

# How did the Jeep get its name?

We're all familiar with the all-purpose Ford vehicle known as the Jeep. Its design began as a contest sponsored by the United States government. A four-wheel-drive vehicle that was practical, easy to drive, and could carry at least a quarter-ton load was needed for the army troops of World War II. But the vehicle, however, could not weigh more than 2,160 pounds.

Three automakers submitted designs. One of the companies was Willys-Overland, but they had a problem with the weight—they were 250 pounds over the limit. At the last minute, they revised their vehicle to make it lighter. The revisions were so close that only one coat of paint could be put on their prototype. The second coat would have made the vehicle too heavy. In the end, the army used a Jeep that was a combination of all three designs from Ford, Willys, and American Bantam.

Its many abilities may have helped lead to the Jeep name. The vehicle was first used as a reconnaissance car by the army in 1940, and it arrived with the letters *GP* painted on its side. The letters stood for "General Purpose," and many people claim that the name was a shortened version of those initials. Others, however, point to the Popeye cartoon character whose name was Eugene the Jeep. Appearing in comic strips during the late 1930s, he was a little creature who ate orchids, solved problems, and could do almost anything.

Whichever of the two possibilities really gave the Jeep its name, one thing was certain—it was indeed depended on for a variety of purposes. During the war, one Jeep that was completely buried by sand in a desert and another that traveled underwater tied to a submarine were still very much drivable when they were recovered.

People were impressed by the Jeep because it was so dependable. It was also versatile, which meant that it could be counted on to perform well in a variety of situations. If that's what we're looking for in a vehicle, doesn't it make sense that we'd look for those same qualities, only magnified, in our God? Dependability and versatility are exactly what you get from God—guaranteed. Lifetime warranty, and beyond! God makes this promise to you: "I will never, never fail you nor forsake you" (Hebrews 13:5). You even have his promise in writing—just check your Bible for the contract.

## 86

# When did a painting turn into a puzzle?

First, the painting disappeared completely. It was called *St. Jerome,* by Leonardo da Vinci, and it was owned by a painter named Angelica Kauffman. When she died in 1804, the painting was discovered to be missing. For 10 years the mystery went unsolved.

Then Cardinal Joseph Fesch, while pursuing his hobby of touring through the antique shops of Rome, stumbled across a box. Its lid was made from the painting of St. Jerome, but the section containing Jerome's head was missing. The cardinal bought the box anyway. A few months later, in another shop, Cardinal Fesch found a head that looked similar to the one missing from his painting. When he took it home, he was excited to see that it matched exactly. The pieces of the puzzle were finally reunited for posterity.

The odds of rejoining both pieces of art were very slim. Yet it happened. Maybe you've strayed far from Jesus, and you think there's no way to get back. But putting things back together is Jesus' specialty. No matter how far away you are or how long you've been hidden, if you want to join Jesus again, he can find you. The Bible says, "I will seek my lost ones, those who strayed away, and bring them safely home again. I will put splints and bandages upon their broken limbs and heal the sick" (Ezekiel 34:15-16). Tell Jesus that you're lost, and he will make you whole again.

**87**

# How did marketing make Kleenex successful?

The Kimberly-Clark Company had a problem. During World War I, they had supplied the soldiers with Cellucotton, a tissue made from a mixture of cotton and wood fibers. Cellucotton was used for dressing wounds and as a filter for gas masks. After the war, a huge quantity of Cellucotton remained. What could be done with it?

Kimberly-Clark decided to present the tissues to the American public as a glamorous, "scientific" way to remove makeup. Many celebrities were used in the advertising campaign, and sales slowly but steadily increased. Kimberly-Clark was very surprised to receive a great deal of mail regarding their Cellucotton. Wives were reporting that their husbands were taking their makeup tissues to use as handkerchiefs. Men were wondering why the product wasn't being advertised as a disposable hankie.

Meanwhile, Andrew Olsen invented a new pop-up tissue box in 1921, which Kimberly-Clark began to use. The box was called Serv-a-Tissue, and it increased sales even more. Some officials at Kimberly-Clark wanted to keep Cellucotton as a makeup remover, but others wanted to market it as a disposable handkerchief. To settle the dispute, they went to Peoria, Illinois, to decide. The people there were given two coupons—one for the makeup tissue, one for the nose-blowing tissue. More people noticed and turned in the coupons for free hankies, and that was the official birth of Kleenex.

It's amazing how many products throughout history have become successful because they filled a need. It took the people of the Kimberly-Clark Company six years to figure out what need they were attempting to fill, and that was after repeated requests from the public. You will never have that problem with God. The Bible tells us, "Remember, your Father knows exactly what you need even before you ask him!" (Matthew 6:8). No human is capable of caring so completely. God is the only one who can.

---

# 88
# How did a photographer's pictures change children's lives?

A camera can change people's lives. Lewis Hine knows how powerful a camera can be because his pictures altered the lives of all American children. Hine was hired by the National Child Labor Committee to photograph children at work.

In the early 1900s, children, many under 14 years old, were forced to work in mines or factories to help support their poverty-stricken families. A 14-hour workday was not unusual. Hine went to the West Virginia glass factories, the New England canneries, and the Southern cotton mills, taking pictures that showed the cruelty and hardships children endured. Guilty of exploiting the children, business owners felt very threatened by the photographer. He was not welcome in many places.

On one occasion, Hine was riding on a train when it suddenly stopped. A group of men approached him with hot tar and feathers. Hine said he knew that the men wanted to "cover me with tar and feathers and turn me into a turkey." Fortunately, it was a ruse. The men secretly wanted to help

Hine escape from some real enemies. They took him off the train to safety. Because of Lewis Hine's pictures, America finally made a law against child labor in 1938.

Lewis Hine taught most of America to look at its children through new eyes, in a new way. After they saw a better way, they acted on it. That's how a relationship with God works. We ask him, "Open my eyes to see wonderful things in your Word" (Psalm 119:18). Once we see a picture of how much better our life can become when God is in charge, we feel the need to act by inviting God to take over. Read God's Word for yourself, and he will make many things clear.

## 89
# Is it possible to learn a language overnight?

Joseph Caspar Mezzofanti always had something to say. He was a talented communicator, who by age 12 could already speak eight different languages. The Italian boy wanted to be a priest, but he wasn't old enough. He decided to study more languages until he was ordained. In 1833 the pope called Joseph to the Vatican, where he served as head librarian before being promoted to a cardinal. Through it all, Joseph became well known for his ability to understand the confessions of foreign prisoners.

The cardinal's most impressive achievement involved two

foreigners who were scheduled for execution the next day. Joseph prepared himself by learning their whole language in just one night so that they could speak to him freely before their death. In total, Joseph knew 38 languages perfectly. He learned Chinese, the most difficult, in only four months. Joseph understood or partially spoke another 50 languages. Most amazing of all, he had never left the country of Italy, where he was born.

The fact that Joseph could communicate with so many people was amazing. It didn't matter so much what he said—people were just impressed that he could say it at all. If Joseph was amazing, God is astounding. God speaks to every man on earth, and every single person knows exactly what God is saying. But in addition, the Bible tells us, "The Lord grants wisdom! His every word is a treasure of knowledge and understanding" (Proverbs 2:6). God is the perfect communicator, and listening to him will give you the truth.

---

## 90
# How do you address people with the same name?

Imagine being in a crowded room, where you could only talk about someone by using his first name. There are four "Jeffreys" present. How can you say which one you mean without going into a long description of how he looks or what he's doing?

In early history, people experienced this confusion when only first names were used. As the population grew, there were too many people with the same name. Another kind of reference was needed, and that's how last names came about. At first, last names were especially popular with nobility—the wealthier people—because they were trying to separate themselves from the common people. Eventually, everyone used the "surname," an added name derived from an occupation or other circumstance.

Which last name you were assigned could depend on several things. If your father was named John, your last name might be Johnson. If you have a *Mc* or *Mac* at the beginning of your name, that also stands for "son of." *MacGregor* means "son of Gregory." You could be named for where you lived. Living near the village green could earn you the name Peter Green. They might name you for how you look: Robert Longfellow or Cathy Small or chestnut-haired Sally Brown.

Then there's what you did for a living: You could be Tom Baker if you worked with bread, Greg Mason if you worked with bricks, Sam Taylor if you worked with clothes, or John Smith if you were a blacksmith. Some last names have become harder to trace than others, but originally each of your ancestors probably had a very good reason for the name they have passed on to you.

We use names as a way of identifying who someone is and what he does. God knows that we rely on names for information, so he gives us several names to call him. He wants us to know who he is and what he can do for us. The

Bible says, "He will be called Wonderful Counselor, Mighty God, Everlasting Father, Prince of Peace" (Isaiah 9:6, NIV).

We all would love to find a wonderful counselor, someone we can confide in and depend on. We'd welcome having connections with someone mighty when we're feeling weak. It would be so comforting to have an everlasting father to guide and protect us, and who doesn't need more peace? The Prince of Peace can supply it abundantly. Knowing that names are descriptions, what more do you need to know about God?

## 91

# How could you commit a crime with a pillow?

You've been sleeping on a new pillow, but the crackling from the tag is driving you crazy. You decide to cut it off. Suddenly you see those words again: "Do not remove under penalty of law." What will happen if you snip it with the scissors? Will the police or the FBI come knocking on your door? Will cutting the tag cause some kind of unforeseen harm to the pillow or to you?

Don't worry or lose any sleep. The warning on the tag isn't even directed at you. It's addressed to the manufacturers and sellers of your pillow. Some time ago the people who stuffed upholstered articles didn't always use the materials they were supposed to. The tag was meant to make them comply with safety laws.

The law insists that the contents of your purchase be listed on the tag so that you'll know what you're buying. The sellers are the ones who aren't allowed to remove it. The tag that seemed such a threat to you is actually there for your protection. Once you take your purchase home, you may do whatever you'd like with the tag. Newer tags, by the way, now say, "Under penalty of law this tag is not to be removed, except by the consumer."

These tags have been a little intimidating to some of us. If a threat from a pillow can make us take notice, why aren't we paying much more attention to a message that comes straight from God? He has said, "If you have ears, listen! And be sure to put into practice what you hear. The more you do this, the more you will understand what I tell you" (Mark 4:23-24). God wants you to focus on a real danger—that you'll miss out on a lifetime of blessings. The next time you lay your head on your pillow, don't worry about the tag. Instead, concentrate on a label for yourself: "Do not remove from God."

## 92

# What's so great about grass?

Toward the end of summer you may be wondering just exactly whose idea it was to plant grass all around a house. Actually, yards have existed since 400 B.C., but grass was only used as a background to contrast and accentuate the garden and flowers. Until the 1800s, long grass combined with wild-flowers was admired. But you can thank nineteenth century Europe for starting the idea of manicuring yards.

Rich and poor alike enjoyed lawn games like golf and bowling, so both castles and cottages were surrounded with pretty playing fields. Besides, low grass made it easier to see who was approaching, serving as an early warning of intrud-ers. Much later, as people began moving into the suburbs, they were anxious to match their neighbors' yards, and grassy lawns became a status symbol.

In early history, unless you had a flock of sheep that could constantly gnaw the lawn, grass had to be cut with a scythe. Then, in the 1820s, Edwin Budding invented a rotary push mower. The large version was horse drawn and not popular because the divots from the horses' hooves ruined the job. The small, human-powered push mower was gradually accepted. It was almost 100 years later before Edwin George took the engine from his wife's washing machine and attached it to the back of his mower, creating the first gas-powered version.

As for the topsoil you spread to keep your grass healthy, con-sider this: It takes 500 to 600 years for just a one-inch layer to accumulate from clay, sand, and the remains of decayed ani-mals and plants. Like it or not, your lawn care is more than a time-consuming chore—it's a creation of man and nature.

If you stopped taking care of your lawn, it would eventu-ally decay, die, and return back to dirt. The rains would come and wash the dirt away, and the wind would blow away the dust. The Bible says, "The grass withers, the flowers fade, but the Word of our God shall stand forever" (Isaiah 40:8). Sometimes we may end up spending more time taking care of our yard than our soul. Estimate your efforts, and make adjustments now if you need to. It doesn't make much sense to nourish and cultivate the outside if the "inside" is in danger of drying up and withering away.

## 93

# What lieutenant wouldn't stop fighting World War II?

You have to admire the man for his obedience. Japanese Lieutenant Hiroo Onoda was ordered not to surrender to the enemy during World War II. He didn't—even 30 years after the war was over. Onoda was left by his countrymen on the Philippine Islands with the promise that they would come back. The war ended, Japan surrendered, and papers were dropped on the island explaining to their soldiers that they should come out of the jungle.

But Onoda thought the announcements were a trick and ignored them. He lived in the jungle from 1945 to 1974, until a young Japanese explorer told the loyal lieutenant that the war was over. Even then Onoda wouldn't believe it. He said he would only surrender after receiving word from his former commanding officer. Fortunately, the man was still alive. He was brought to the island, and only then did Onoda accept the truth.

Because Onoda stayed hidden, he missed years and years of a better life. He made things much harder on himself than they had to be. Sometimes we think that if we hide from God, we will be better off. We sometimes make the mistake of thinking of God as our enemy. But the Bible says, "There is nothing concealed that will not be disclosed, or hidden that will not be made known. What you have said in the dark will be heard in the daylight, and what you have whispered in the ear in the inner rooms will be proclaimed from the roofs" (Luke 12:2-3, NIV).

It is impossible to hide from God. God already knows the worst things about you, and yet he promises to love you no matter what you have done. If you are weary of ducking, dodging, and hiding, come out into the freedom of the pure light of God's love by asking his forgiveness. He will give you a clean soul and a fresh start.

---

## 94

# Why did one letter take seven years to reach the White House?

During the Vietnam War, a soldier named George Mellendorf was distressed about how long it was taking to send and receive his letters. At that time, travel and communication were difficult. Nevertheless, George decided to try to do something about it. He went straight to the top, sending a letter of complaint to the president of the United States, Richard Milhous Nixon. George's letter said:

"Dear President Nixon: It seems nobody cares if we get our mail. We are lucky to get it twice a week. Sir, someone is not doing their job."

George didn't get an answer to his letter, written in January of 1971, that year or the next or the next. Apparently, everything possible was already being done to improve the mail service, but things still remained tough. George's letter didn't actually arrive at the White House until 1978, more than seven years after it was sent.

Surely George was hoping that he would get a fast answer to his letter. It probably crossed his mind that he was not important enough to be "worth" the efforts of the president. Jesus is the most important, most exalted, and highest ranking person who ever existed. But you never have to worry about getting his attention.

You have his promise to count on, and Jesus never goes back on his word. He said, "Ask, and you will be given what you ask for. Seek, and you will find. Knock, and the door will be opened. For everyone who asks, receives. Anyone who seeks, finds. If only you will knock, the door will open" (Matthew 7:7-8). You are so important to God that he will always answer you. If you haven't already, ask him to open the door to his kingdom for you, and see for yourself.

# What did you get if you ordered "bossy in a bowl"?

If a waitress brought you "bossy in a bowl," "dog biscuits," and "nervous pudding," what would you be eating? Beef stew, crackers, and Jell-O! Before restaurants became so crowded, waitresses didn't write down your order—they just announced it to the cook over the counter. There was a special language that spiced up the restaurant routine, and its nickname was "hash house Greek." Descriptions for certain foods were made up, and everyone who worked in the restaurant knew which was which. "Moo juice" was milk, "brown cow" was chocolate milk, cereal was a "bowl of birdseed," and a sandwich "with grass" meant it came with lettuce. As more people began eating out, orders were streamlined, and dining became more efficient. But no one can deny that it's much less colorful.

Names are important. They're what we use when we're trying to communicate an idea. The most important of all names, of course, is Jesus. He says, "All around the world they will offer sweet incense and pure offerings in honor of my name. For my name shall be great among the nations" (Malachi 1:11). If you didn't live in the "diner" generation or eat out a lot, you might never have heard of their strange names for food. Maybe that makes you feel like you missed out on a fun time in America. In all generations and in all places, Jesus will be known. You'll only miss out if you don't ask him in.

## 96

# What is the surprise ingredient in your cereal?

Since our bodies need iron to help oxygen get to our muscles, many cereals are becoming "iron-fortified"—and they really mean it. Did you know, however, that you are actually eating pieces of iron on a regular basis? It's added to cereal in the form of tiny metal filings. You can even see the slivers by taking a very strong magnet and plunging it into the box. The magnet will attract these specks, and you'll be able to inspect them. Although it doesn't sound very appetizing, eating the metal shavings is harmless.

God was the one who designed metal to be attracted to a magnet. He could have, if he had wanted to, made us unable to resist him by creating us to be pulled to him against our will. But God gave us hearts and souls and emotions, which make us different from mere animals. He also gave us the will to choose. If we become attracted to God, it is because we realize that he has something that we need. God says, "I have loved you with an everlasting love; I have

drawn you with loving-kindness" (Jeremiah 31:3, NIV).
Draw near to the only source that can fortify your life with
true loving-kindness.

―――――――――――――――― 97

# When was delivering mail a challenge for mailmen?

In the early 1900s it was a real challenge to be a
mail carrier. Driving up to a country house, the mailman
never knew where he'd be putting the mail. He could find
any type of container—an ordinary basket, or even something a little more imaginative, like an old tire or a cigar box
or an oil can. At each stop, the mailman had to leave his
truck, hunt for the place, and hope that the rain or snow
didn't destroy letters that weren't protected from the weather.

In 1902 Congress authorized a standard-size mailbox, but
the postmaster general had to sift through proposed plans
for the next 13 years before postal worker Roy Joroleman
came up with the winning design seen everywhere today.

That doesn't mean that mail carriers always have it easy
now. People still find ways to modify their mailboxes. Lee
Patterson of Montana built his box 14 feet in the air. As a
basketball player, he enjoyed jumping for his letters. The
postman, however, wasn't thrilled about having to stand on
the roof of his truck to complete his job.

We depend on mail carriers to deliver messages to us. You've probably waited anxiously for the mail at least once, anticipating something important. Have you ever been that eager to read the Bible? It contains the most important written words of your life because its message has the greatest meaning.

The Bible says, "Jesus' disciples saw him do many other miracles besides the ones told about in this book, but these are recorded so that you will believe that he is the Messiah, the Son of God, and that believing in him you will have life" (John 20:30-31). God wants you to enjoy and cherish his words in the Bible. It was sent special delivery just for you.

## 98

# What can happen if you only have one copy of your manuscript?

Before the days of copiers and computers, writing could be a risky business. Take Thomas Carlyle, for instance. He had written a book called *The French Revolution*. He wanted his good friend's opinion, so he sent the manuscript to John Stuart Mill for review. Mill had to leave his house for a time, and while he was gone, the maid lit a fire in the grate. What did she use for fuel? The manuscript, of course, which she thought was scratch paper. Thomas Carlyle had to rewrite the whole book.

Then there was the English poet Dante Gabriel Rossetti. When his beloved wife died in 1862, he was so grief-stricken and distraught that he placed his only copy of a manuscript of love sonnets in her coffin. Long after she had been buried, Dante decided he needed the manuscript back, so he had his wife exhumed. The poems were subsequently published at a later date.

These men's works were vulnerable because they were made by humans, with the weaknesses and faults that all men have. Don't depend on anything unless it comes from God. God is the only one who can promise, "Heaven and earth will pass away, but my words will never pass away" (Matthew 24:35, NIV). The Bible has the only words that were available yesterday, are available today, and will be available tomorrow.

## 99

# How did foot powder win a mayoral race?

Advertising can be powerful. In 1969 there was an election for mayor in a town in Ecuador. Newspapers began running an ad for Pulvapies foot powder that looked just like a voting ballot. The ads made it look like the can of foot powder was a candidate for the mayor's race. They said, "Vote for Pulvapies" and "Vote for any candidate, but if you want well-being and hygiene, vote for Pulvapies." People did. So many people used the fake ballots that the foot powder won the election!

Elections help us express our opinions about how we would like our future to be. There is a much more important choice you must make, one that will affect you for all eternity. The Bible says, "If serving the Lord seems undesirable to you, then choose for yourselves this day whom you will serve" (Joshua 24:15, NIV). Will you vote for life everlasting in heaven with Jesus or for the fleeting fame or wealth that you might attain here on earth by following some person or doctrine that doesn't include God? Elect to live your life with Christ at its center.

# 100

# Why would a house have 2,000 doors?

If there were a prize for "Strangest House in America," the Winchester mansion in California would probably win. It was owned by Sarah Winchester, who had inherited the fortune made by her father-in-law from the Winchester Repeating Arms Company, which was famous for its rifles.

Winchester was plagued by the fear that she was being visited by the souls of people who had been shot by her family's guns. She thought that these souls wouldn't be able to find her if she made her house confusing enough, so renovations and construction were daily happenings at the Winchester house for 38 years. What was being built?

Doors that led to brick walls, stairways that didn't go anywhere, and windows that showed no view. There were 160 rooms with 48 fireplaces that took up eight stories and six acres. The final total was 10,000 windows and 2,000 doors by the time Winchester died at age 85 in 1922.

The Winchester house was built from the motivations of fear, dread, and anxiety. All of those many rooms provided no comfort or sense of security to Winchester. Jesus talked about his Father's house, which is also a mansion. He said, "In my Father's house are many rooms; if it were not so, I would have told you. I am going there to prepare a place for you. And if I go and prepare a place for you, I will come back and take you to be with me that you also may be where I am. You know the way to the place where I am going" (John 14:2-4, NIV). We can't know for sure what God's house will be like until we get there, but we can be certain that it was built out of love. In his mansion no fear, despair, dread, or anxiety will even exist.

## 101

# How did a nose and some fingertips help make measurements?

Where would you go to see the one, the only, the original metric meter? One actually does exist, and it's kept in Paris. It's made of platinum alloy, and all meters around the world are measured to its markings.

We can thank Napoleon for the metric system. He wanted to find a way to unite all the countries he had conquered so that the people would have something in common. Napoleon's scientists devised the meter by determining that it was one 10-millionth of the distance between the North Pole and the equator. They weren't completely exact with that calculation, but they did establish a length everyone could use.

The meter was a big improvement on the yard, which King Henry VIII declared to be precisely the distance between the tip of his (and only his) nose and the tips of his outstretched fingers. An inch was supposed to be the width of a thumb—any thumb. You can see the problem. A foot was as long as a person's foot, and a cubit, which was an even older measurement, was the length between the elbow to the tip of the middle finger. The word *meter* comes from the Greek word *metron*, which means "measure." The meter made measuring a lot simpler for everyone.

No matter what we try to measure, our efforts will always

fall short compared to God's standard. The Bible says, "Who else has held the oceans in his hands and measured off the heavens with his ruler? Who else knows the weight of all the earth and weighs the mountains and the hills?" (Isaiah 40:12). As humans, we can only measure those things that God has already created. His might is beyond measure!

# 102

# Why does metal feel colder than wood?

Have you noticed that whenever you touch a piece of metal, it feels cool? Try it now by feeling a doorknob, and then the door. What makes the difference in the temperature? Metal is a good conductor of heat, which means that heat moves through it quickly. When you touch metal, it immediately pulls heat from your hand. This makes your skin feel cool. It's not really that metal itself is cold. It's just better at taking heat away from you.

God uses an example about temperature to teach us how to live. He says, "I know your deeds, that you are neither cold nor hot. I wish you were either one or the other! So, because you are lukewarm—neither hot nor cold—I am about to spit you out of my mouth. You say, 'I am rich; I have acquired wealth and do not need a thing.' But you do not realize that you are wretched, pitiful, poor, blind and naked. I counsel you to buy from me gold refined in the fire, so you can become rich; and white clothes to wear, so you can cover your shameful nakedness; and salve to put on your eyes, so you can see" (Revelation 3:15-18, NIV).

God wants you to commit yourself to him so that he can give you riches, purity, and wisdom of the soul. It is the one decision that will never leave you cold.

# 103

# What billion-dollar industry was created from paper cups and milk shakes?

Ray Kroc was a paper cup salesman. He tried to think of more ways for people to fill his cups. When he learned about a machine called a Multimixer, which made malted milk shakes, Ray began selling those. That's how he ran across the McDonald brothers, who were running a hamburger stand that used eight Multimixers—enough to make 40 milk shakes at once! Ray visited the restaurant in California to see how it was being run, and he was very impressed.

Dick and Mac McDonald were brothers who had figured out a great system for selling hamburgers. Unlike most res-taurants, they didn't use carhops or have dishes that had to be washed. They offered a limited menu of nine items at reasonable prices so that the food could be ready to go: Hamburgers were 15¢, french fries were 10¢, and milk shakes were 20¢. There was a platter that spun to toast 24 buns at the same time. The staff was all male, and each man had one specific job to do. The restaurant was spotlessly clean. Their mascot was a little man named Speedee, but he was soon dropped because he looked so much like the Alka-Seltzer mascot. In 1955 the new symbol became the "golden arches."

Prior to that, in 1954, Ray began franchising the McDonald's concept in exchange for giving the brothers a percentage of these new restaurants' sales. He had even asked the brothers why they didn't build more McDonald's restaurants themselves. They said that they had all the money they needed, and they just didn't want the headaches that came with expanding.

Under Ray's direction, the first new McDonald's opened in Des Plaines, Illinois, in 1955. In 1958 a designer of submarine kitchens was hired to design the most efficient restaurants possible. A special metal scoop for french fries was developed. The air-conditioning systems were so advanced that all the air in the restaurants was renewed every three minutes. Every manager and owner of a McDonald's restaurant earned a degree of "Bachelor of Hamburgerology."

Although Ray Kroc had many successes, not everything he thought of was wonderful. He once tried to sell a grilled pineapple-and-cheese sandwich called the "Hulaburger." In 1961 the brothers sold all McDonald's rights to Ray. Despite the fact that Ray Kroc became a rich man, neither Dick nor Mac McDonald ever expressed regret at selling their fast-food concept.

The McDonald brothers seemed to have been doubly

wise. They came up with a winning combination for selling
fast food. But even more valuable was their decision not to
be involved in the expansion of McDonald's. The rest of the
world may say that the brothers were misguided. They could
have been zillionaires! But they were already richer than
they appeared because they had learned a lesson that
money can't buy.

The Bible says, "Keep your life free from love of money,
and be content with what you have" (Hebrews 13:5, RSV).
Sometimes, don't you get tired of the hustle and bustle of
living in the "fast lane"? God wants us to know that we
aren't required to push so hard. We're allowed to take the
time to count our blessings instead of our bucks.

# 104

# What popular game began on the grounds of a hotel?

If you were visiting Carter's Lookout Mountain
Hotel in Tennessee in 1926, you could do something that
no one else in America had ever done before. Garnet Carter,
the hotel's owner, had just invented this activity for his
guests. No one could guess what a popular fad it would
become or how profitable it would be. What was keeping
the residents of the hotel so busy? Miniature golf, which Carter called "Tom Thumb" golf after the midget in the P. T. Bar-

num circus. When Carter saw how many people wanted to play, he started the Fairyland Manufacturing Company, which made courses at other locations in one week's time for $2,000. By 1930, 200,000 people were working in the miniature golf industry. People began to think that this was an easy way to get rich quick, and soon there were so many golf courses that players became bored with the game, and the fad died—except as a children's amusement.

The public can be fickle. They can love something, hate something, or seesaw back and forth between the two. Whenever you're trying to anticipate what the public wants, don't put your trust completely in what appears to be true at the moment. In fact, throughout life you really can't trust anything to be absolutely unchangeable except God's love for you. The Bible says, "Jesus Christ is the same yesterday, today, and forever" (Hebrews 13:8). You never have to worry about fads, cycles, or trends with God's love. It will never fade.

## 105

# Why did the richest woman in the world eat cold oatmeal?

What would you do if you inherited $10 million? Hetty Green, the daughter of a shipping magnate, found herself in that position. She decided to make it grow, and she succeeded, acquiring $100 million by the time she died in 1916. But becoming the richest woman in the world had its cost.

Hetty married a millionaire, from whom she separated because he spent too much money. He died bankrupt, with only a pocket watch and seven dollars. Hetty was just as hard on her children. They were forced to wear rags. Her daughter was sent away to live in a convent and become a nun because then her expenses would be paid for by the nuns.

When Hetty's son's leg became infected, she wouldn't take him to a doctor. She took him to the charity ward at the hospital instead. When Hetty was recognized, she refused to pay and took her son home without treatment. Later his leg had to be amputated. Even then Hetty wouldn't pay for a hospital stay. She insisted that the operation be performed in her house.

Hetty ate cold oatmeal, onions, and cold eggs rather than pay for fuel to heat her food. She once spent hours searching the street for a coin her son had lost. She sold her newspapers to someone else for half-price after she read them. Rather than spend money on an office, Hetty surrounded herself with her ragtag trunks and papers and sat on the floor in the middle of her bank building to conduct her business. She wore rubber boots with money stuffed in them and a dirty black dress. She worried constantly about people trying to take her money. By the time she died, Hetty had earned herself a nickname because of her miserly methods. She was called "The Witch of Wall Street."

The Bible says, "If you must choose, take a good name rather than great riches; for to be held in loving esteem is better than silver and gold" (Proverbs 22:1). Although we can't sit in judgment of Hetty, from all appearances, she didn't lead a pleasant life even though she had lots of money. She put her money ahead of her son's health and comfort, as well as her own. She was not beloved by those who knew her. We can only speculate on how much good her money could have done for so many people, including Hetty's own family. The fact that Hetty left behind great riches and an unflattering nickname seems to show that she wasn't as happy as she could have been if she had lived with her values the other way around.

## 106

# Why did Moses have horns on his head?

Moses should be pictured with rays of light coming from his head, but instead he has horns. How did that happen? Michelangelo made his famous sculpture of Moses based on the Bible's description. The problem was that the people translating the Bible from the Hebrew language made a mistake. The Hebrew word for "ray of light" is spelled exactly the same way as the Hebrew word for "horn." The translators chose the wrong word, and that's why the Bible says *horns* and why Moses looks more like the devil than like the man of God he really was.

People who only saw the picture of Moses with horns might doubt his loyalty to God. But the people who knew him could surely tell where his loyalty was. Maybe sometimes in the depths of your heart you wonder about where you stand. Maybe you haven't been within the protection of Jesus for a very long time. But that doesn't mean you belong to the devil.

The Bible tells us how to conquer the devil. It says, "Submit yourselves, then, to God. Resist the devil, and he will flee from you. Come near to God and he will come near to you. Wash your hands, you sinners, and purify your hearts, you double-minded. Grieve, mourn and wail. Change your laughter to mourning and your joy to gloom. Humble yourselves before the Lord, and he will lift you up" (James 4:7-10, NIV). If this whole process sounds too rigorous, remember that the devil is not going to want to give you up without a fight. Ask Jesus to intervene on your behalf, and he will come to rescue you.

## 107

# What American pastime started with a garage door and a projector?

What was Richard Hollingshead Jr. doing in his driveway that night in Camden, New Jersey, in 1932? He had put a screen in front of his garage door, fastened a projector to the top of his car, and then sat in the front seat to watch home movies. That's how the first drive-in movie was born. Hollingshead began planning to market his new idea. He tested his car under a sprinkler to make sure the movie could be seen in the rain, and he planned to serve snacks. In 1933 he began building his dream. His "Automobile Movie Theatre" had parking for 400 cars on a lot the size of a football field. Guardrails kept the cars from rolling off the seven slanting rows. The drive-in was a big success.

After the Great Depression, people loved movies as an escape from their dreary lives and gladly paid the one-dollar fee per car. The biggest problem Hollingshead had to overcome was the sound for the movie. In the beginning, small speakers were placed on the ground under each car, but the sound coming through the floorboards wasn't satisfactory. Next, big speakers on each side of the screen let everyone hear—even those in the neighborhood who didn't want to listen. Finally, speakers that could be hung on car windows proved to be a success.

In the 1950s there were more than 5,000 outdoor theaters. But when television appeared on the scene, people stopped going to drive-ins so regularly. While there are still a few drive-in theaters, they've lost the widespread popularity they once enjoyed.

It's not easy being a trendsetter. People tend to think you're odd and often don't hesitate to point that out. But if you have a good idea, pursue it. God may be speaking to your heart.

The Bible says, "Be sure to use the abilities God has given you. . . . Put these abilities to work so that everyone may notice your improvement and progress. Keep a close watch on all you do and think. Stay true to what is right and God will bless you and use you to help others" (1 Timothy 4:14-16). Work hard, pray hard, and expect big results.

## 108

# How did the term *hangnail* happen?

It's one of those annoying little problems that everyone has experienced. Sometimes on the sides of your fingernails extra bits of skin stick out. We call them "hangnails." If you're thinking, like most of us, that the name comes from the skin hanging from your fingernail, you'd be incorrect.

We all notice hangnails. They take up such a tiny amount of space, but they deliver an attention-getting sting. The name comes from the Old English words for a corn on the toe: *ang*, which stood for "pain," and *naegl*, which meant "nail," because they thought the corn looked like the head of a nail. After a while, the words blurred together in sound, and the meaning grew to include fingers.

When a hangnail is hurting us, we know what to do about it. But sometimes the hurt doesn't come from a place you can pinpoint. You just know it's a dull, sad ache in your heart. God knows about that feeling, and he knows how to fix it. He wants you to say, "When I sit in darkness, the Lord himself will be my Light" (Micah 7:8). Let him blow away the clouds of gloom that are stinging your heart and keeping you from feeling joyful. He will be your companion and your comforter, and he'll help you find a brighter tomorrow.

# How did a captive audience escape from the singing emperor?

You would think that being emperor of Rome would be enough for any man. But not so for Nero. His most-desired goal was to become a singer. He took lessons and then chose to have his first recital in Naples, where things did not go well. The earth shook with a tremor during the performance, and several people left while Nero was still singing.

Apparently used to more loyalty than this, Nero arranged to have the gates locked so that his future audiences would be sure to stay. Some of the men got so tired of applauding, they jumped over the walls. A woman was not so fortunate—she gave birth in the stands. Three other men came up with a creative plan to get the guards to let them out of the gates. One man played dead, and the other two volunteered to carry him out.

Nero tried to force his singing on people, but it didn't work. You can't make someone like you. But when you are right with God, you will be given some tools to attract people. The Bible says, "The fruit of the Spirit is love, joy, peace, patience, kindness, goodness, faithfulness, gentleness, and self-control" (Galatians 5:22-23, NIV). We'd all enjoy

working with, living next to, or spending time with someone who had these qualities. Let God develop these qualities in you.

# 110

# Where would you find a nest egg?

You're trying to save money, so you tell your friends
you're making a nice little nest egg for yourself. Unless
you're a farmer, you may not be aware that there really is
such a thing as a nest egg, and it has nothing to do with
money.

Long ago farmers who raised chickens would put a fake
egg, sometimes made of porcelain, in the nest with the hen.
This was supposed to induce her to lay more eggs than she
otherwise would. We've borrowed the term and the idea. If
we put a little money away, maybe it will turn into more as
we get used to adding to it.

It's good to put money aside, but it's not so good if accumulating money is what you care about most. Don't forget
the value of friendship and sharing and loving and giving.
The joys and blessings that come from caring about others
are precious. Collect people as vigorously as you collect pen-
nies. The Bible talks about keeping a balance. It says, "Wherever your treasure is, there your heart and thoughts will also
be" (Luke 12:34). If you count your treasure in the love that
you give and receive, you'll always be wealthy in spirit.

# III

# When was *Heidi* the most unpopular movie on television?

Imagine that you're the television executive in charge of making a programming decision. You've been broadcasting a football game. There's one minute and five seconds left in the game. The score is 32 to 29. A movie is scheduled to begin in one minute. What will it be—the end of the football game or the beginning of *Heidi*?

One unfortunate executive made the wrong choice in 1968 during the Oakland Raiders–New York Jets game. Viewers called the station trying to figure out why the football players had disappeared and the Alps had come into view. The fans might have been a little more forgiving had they never found out through hearsay what happened in that last crucial minute on the football field.

The Oakland Raiders, who had been behind, made two touchdowns and won the game. Fourteen years later, that game still stood as a gigantic blunder of sports broadcasting. *Sports Illustrated* magazine memorialized it yet again by singling out 1982's worst sports program by giving it the "Heidi Award."

The hard thing about making a decision is that it comes with a result. It's obvious that the programmer who decided to show *Heidi* wasn't very popular for an awfully long time.

There is a big decision for you to make that will affect the rest of your life. You need to choose whether to follow Jesus or not. If you decide that you will, the result will be spectacular.

"'Because he loves me,' says the Lord, 'I will rescue him; I will protect him, for he acknowledges my name. He will call upon me, and I will answer him; I will be with him in trouble, I will deliver him and honor him. With long life will I satisfy him and show him my salvation'" (Psalm 91:14-16, NIV). Making the decision to follow Jesus will bring you everlasting joy that will be far more satisfying than watching a winning touchdown.

# 112
# What's so bad about good news?

Once upon a time there was a newspaper that actually put its emphasis on *good* news. It was part of an experiment that took place in 1900. For one week, Dr. Charles M. Sheldon, a clergyman, took over as editor-in-chief of a Kansas newspaper. Sheldon had already written the best-selling book *In His Steps,* or *What Would Jesus Do?* which novelized a collection of his sermons.

Reporters from all over America came to the offices of the *Topeka Daily Capital* to see what would happen to the paper under Sheldon's guidance. First, changes in the offices were made: Drinking, smoking, and bad language were no longer allowed. The paper didn't accept advertising from questionable or objectionable sponsors. Stories about social occasions and crime were moved to the back pages of the newspaper. The front page contained uplifting editorials and news about how the world could be made a better place. For example, one story told of a famine in India and asked people to help. More than $1 million was collected and sent to Bombay. How did the public react to the newspaper's new image? In that week daily circulation increased from 15,000 copies to 367,000 copies sold.

This story shows one of the truths from the Bible, which says, "Good news from far away is like cold water to the thirsty" (Proverbs 25:25). There are still many people who are parched because they haven't had the healing waters of God's love poured over them in a very long time. Share a cup of the living water today with someone who could use some good news.

## 113

# How do the famous Nielson ratings work?

Almost all of us have heard about how the Nielson ratings determine the success of a television show or how expensive the advertising of its sponsors should be. But not many of us are aware of how the Nielson system actually works. Maybe we imagine someone calling households, asking what program is being watched at the moment. We may have a vague picture of families continuously writing a list of their favorite shows. In truth, collections for the Nielson ratings are much more scientific. They're also automatic and impartial.

The company of A. C. Nielson began in 1923 by taking surveys about machinery and equipment used for industry. By 1954 Nielson had developed a system that could provide the television industry with accurate information about just who was watching what and when. Households are picked strictly by their location, based on census figures. Then each person in the house is asked to fill out a form with specifics including age, income, and occupation.

Every person is assigned a personal viewer button, which he pushes each time he begins to watch TV. The viewer buttons are located on small boxed meters that are attached to each television set in the house. Except for identifying themselves, viewers don't have to do anything else. The meter keeps track of which shows, which channel changes, and which times are used. About twice a day the Nielson technicians have their computers collect information from the meters via a special phone line. Every year about 20 percent of the families picked are changed. The longest a family can participate is five years, but anyone who moves or gets tired of participating is allowed to drop out.

When you participate in the Nielson ratings, you're counted among the popular majority. If you're a Christian, that won't always be the case. In fact, you may have to endure unpleasantness. But Jesus says, "When you are reviled and persecuted and lied about because you are my followers—wonderful! Be happy about it! Be very glad! for a tremendous reward awaits you up in heaven" (Matthew 5:11-12).

# Why don't doctors wear white like nurses?

Nurses have worn white throughout history. The color white seems pure and is a reassurance of cleanliness because you can spot any dirtiness immediately. Doctors, on the other hand, have worn a parade of colors.

Surgeons started with white, also, but switched to a spinach green in 1914 when it was decided that red blood against white cloth was needlessly startling and alarming. The green background dulled the red color, but it still looked too harsh under the operating-room lighting that was developed after World War II. The green was toned down at that time to a "misty" color. Around 1960 the color changed again—this time to a "seal blue." Why? The blue color is more photogenic on television monitors, which have become a part of operating rooms as surgeons record their operations for teaching purposes.

Red against white does make a very striking contrast. Maybe that's why God uses these colors as examples when he offers his purity to you. He says, "No matter how deep the stain of your sins, I can take it out and make you as clean as freshly fallen snow. Even if you are stained as red as crimson, I can make you white as wool" (Isaiah 1:18). There is no such thing as being too bad for God to love. Ask him to clear your conscience, clean your soul, and claim your heart.

# 115

## What was the job of the "official uncorker of bottles"?

In an age of high-tech communications, it's hard to imagine relying on something primitive to send a message. But for its time, the message stuffed inside a glass bottle, sealed with a cork, and tossed into the ocean had a pretty good chance of reaching someone.

In 1954 a sunken ship revealed bottles that had held liquid. After 250 years, the liquid was unrecognizable, but the bottles were still in perfect condition—proof of their durability. Speed of travel depended on the currents; bottles have been known to travel up to 100 miles a day. The direction that the bottles traveled was also dependent on the ocean— two bottles once dropped from the same point ended up in two different places: Africa and Nicaragua.

Another time, in 1875, a Canadian ship's crew mutinied, keeping the steward, who could navigate, but killing the other officers. The steward steered toward France, telling the mutineers that they were near Spain. He then secretly dropped bottles over the side of the boat, explaining what had happened. Within days the French authorities boarded the boat and made arrests. The queen of England even received important intelligence information in a bottle but discovered that it had already been opened by a man in

Dover. She promptly made it illegal to retrieve any message unless you were the official uncorker of bottles.

We all feel like those bottles at times—drifting without direction. Any turmoil has the ability to send us off course, helplessly bobbing out of control. We feel powerless to get back on track. We are tossed and battered by circumstances that totally overwhelm us. When this happens, you need help. You need an anchor. The events that have rocked you may not change, but your responses to them can.

You can rely on the assurance that God is with you. The Bible says, "We have this hope as an anchor for the soul, firm and secure" (Hebrews 6:19, NIV). God won't let you smash into a rock and break into a thousand pieces. He won't let you sink to the bottom. With his strength, he will hold you up and hold you close. Surrender yourself to him, and let him anchor you to the solid ground of his promises.

## 116
# What do checkers and cookies have in common?

Americans are actually responsible for two products that we've probably all assumed originated in China. One is the fortune cookie, and the other is the game of Chinese checkers.

The fortune cookie that we're used to, with the paper fortune wrapped in dough, was created in 1918 by George Jung, a Chinese immigrant. He wanted to give the customers in Chinese restaurants something fun to do while they waited for their food to be prepared. Even though in China there was already a custom of putting messages, such as birth announcements, into cakes, and there was also a similar flat wafer cookie, Jung was the one who thought of putting the two ideas together. At first, Jung printed verses from the Bible on the papers. Later, he added predictions, fortunes, and proverbs.

As for Chinese checkers, the game started in England in the nineteenth century. It was called Halma. By the 1930s, Americans were playing the game with some revisions. It is believed that the name "Chinese checkers" came from the star-shaped game board on which colored marbles are moved. Apparently the star reminded people of the star on the design of the Chinese flag. The Chinese people do play Chinese checkers. They were taught by the Americans and Japanese, who learned it from the English.

Human beings have a natural curiosity. We like to know how things got started. If you've found yourself wondering how the world began, you've probably heard two stories. One is that everything fell into place by itself, and the other is that God made it. To find out for sure, consult the only true reference book. The Bible says, "Before anything else existed, there was Christ, with God. . . . He created everything there is—nothing exists that he didn't make" (John 1:1-3). Begin with this truth, and your spiritual life will be started on a firm foundation.

# Why is the Oscar named after a farmer?

The Oscar—that gold statue of a knight standing on a reel of film—is the trophy that entertainers win at the annual Academy Awards ceremony. The winners' names are kept secret until the envelope is opened on stage, and then they are presented with the trophy. But why is the statue named Oscar? It didn't even have a name until 1931.

That's when Oscar Pierce, a wealthy Texas farmer, unwittingly entered the picture. His niece was the librarian for the Academy of Motion Picture Arts and Sciences. One day she casually mentioned that the knight on the statue looked a little like her Uncle Oscar. A newspaper reporter overheard her comment and published a story, including the information that "employees have affectionately dubbed their famous statuette 'Oscar.'" After that, the name became official and has been used ever since. By the way, the period during World War II was the only time the Oscar wasn't made of metal. Because of shortages, the Oscar was still awarded, but it was made of wood.

Years from now Oscar statues will be sitting on a shelf or mantel somewhere, after the actors and actresses who won them have already died. We're not meant to stay on earth forever. Have you thought about where you will be after you die? Jesus tells us. He says, "It is my Father's will that everyone who sees his Son and believes on him should have eternal life—that I should raise him at the Last Day" (John

6:40). When you ask Jesus into your life, a place is saved for you in heaven. That's a lot better than ending up on some dusty shelf!

## 118 — How could someone lose a three-mile-long painting?

Historians still don't know what happened. In the mid-1800s, an artist named John Banvard decided to paint a landscape of the Mississippi River. He wanted to show everything he saw along 1,200 miles of the river. He spent one year rowing, camping, and making sketches. Then he built a studio in Kentucky large enough to accommodate his canvas, which he wound around large spools. It took Banvard five years to complete his painting, which included scenes of Indian settlements, riverboats, a shipwreck, and local forts.

Completed in 1846, the painting was exhibited across America and Britain. People would gather all along the tour to watch Banvard spend two hours unrolling his canvas. The artwork, titled *Panorama of the Mississippi*, was updated through the years. In 1862, for example, the painter added another section depicting part of the Civil War. The wear and tear of traveling caused the landscape to begin deteriorating. Eventually, portions of the painting were cut to make backdrop scenery for theaters. Banvard died in 1891, but no one knows what happened to the rest of his painting after his death. Not one picture remains to show Banvard's contribution to American art.

Everyone was amazed at how large and lifelike Banvard's painting was. But the painting was only a copy of the "real thing" that we see growing and changing around us every day. Isn't a tree that buds more fascinating than one that never changes? And what could be more magnificent in size than the world we walk through every day?

The Bible says, "When I look up into the night skies and see the work of your fingers—the moon and the stars you have made—I cannot understand how you can bother with mere puny man, to pay attention to him!" (Psalm 8:3-4). God not only pays attention to us but also makes it clear that we are his most important creation. What an honor to be the central subjects in God's artistic panorama!

_____ **119**

# Why wasn't the perfect book perfect?

Once a well-regarded publishing house, the University Press of Glasgow, Scotland, set out to publish a completely error-free book. The process was started by six proofreaders, who used their experience to check and recheck every page for mistakes. Next, each page of the book was publicly posted at the University, and a reward was offered to students or faculty members who could find any errors. After two weeks and many corrections, the publishers printed the book, feeling fairly confident that the manu-script was flawless. But they were wrong. Several mistakes appeared in the finished book. The first error was spotted on the first page in the first sentence.

Ever had a day like that? No matter how hard you try to make things go smoothly, something goes wrong from the very first. The alarm doesn't go off. The outfit you're wear-ing for the special presentation at work has a spot on it. The dog is sick. Your normal route to work is narrowed to one lane. The list can be endless. But are you doomed to be battered and tossed around by every event that comes along?

King David in the Bible was struggling, also. First, he tells us about his anxiety. Then we learn what he did about it. Finally, he gives us a prayer to use when we're feeling anx-ious. He starts with: "Who will protect me from the wicked? Who will be my shield? I would have died unless the Lord had helped me. I screamed, 'I'm slipping, Lord!' and he was kind and saved me. Lord, when doubts fill my mind, when my heart is in turmoil, quiet me and give me renewed hope and cheer" (Psalm 94:16-19). God has the perfect way to help us handle our hassles.

# How are "scratch 'n' sniff" products made?

Kids love the bright-colored fruit stickers that smell like oranges, watermelons, and strawberries. The perfume samples handed out at the drugstore or tucked in a magazine are appreciated by women who want to try before they buy. Its technical name is microfragrance or microencapsulation, but it's popularly known as "scratch 'n' sniff." How does it work?

The idea is to keep a fragrance contained until someone wishes to smell it. The people who make scratch 'n' sniff products start with a minuscule plastic capsule, too small to see. The scent is enclosed in the capsules by mixing perfume oil with water to form tiny droplets. These drops are sprinkled on some surface and then are coated with plastic. The droplets are sometimes heated, sometimes left alone, until they have set in the plastic. Then another coat of resin is applied, which sticks the whole thing to paper. When the paper is scratched, or an adhesive seal is broken, the capsules release the fragrance.

The idea was developed in the 1960s by the 3M company. At one time there was even a scratch 'n' sniff movie. Members of the audience were given sheets with numbered samples. When the movie screen showed number three, for example, everyone would scratch sample number three and then smell roses, or popcorn, or whatever scent matched the action in the film.

God made all of our senses, so he knows how pleasant it is for us to smell something fragrant. He meant for us to enjoy our sense of smell and to be delighted with an appealing scent. He uses the following comparison to encourage us to choose kind words: "Friendly suggestions are as pleasant as perfume" (Proverbs 27:9).

You don't ever have to be critical or stern, bossy or spiteful when you speak to someone. If you are, he will be repelled and won't pay attention. Instead, find a way to deliver your message with peaceful words, encouraging words, and words of hope and help. Whoever hears you will listen much more carefully—drawn to your kindness in the same way that he would move toward a fresh cup of hot coffee or some newly baked bread.

## 121

# What were cats once accused of causing?

Between 1334 and 1351 there was an outbreak of bubonic plague, also called the Black Death or Black Plague. As much as 75 percent of Asian and European populations died. How could this have happened? The main problem was that people had no idea how the disease was carried.

At first they were worried that cats were responsible. Thousands of cats were killed in the hopes that the disease would be stopped. But the disease spread faster than ever. Finally people began to realize that killing their cats was the worst possible thing they could have done. The bites of fleas caused the plague. The fleas stayed on rats, and the rat population exploded because the natural predators of rats—the cats—had been eliminated. It was determined that all garbage should be burned every day. That way there was less to attract the rats. This practice eventually allowed the disease to fade away.

During the time of the plague, the people didn't know what to do. They panicked and selected the most disastrous course of action. Maybe that has happened to you. Perhaps you are so overwhelmed by what's happening to you that you don't know which way to turn. You've tried to fix the problem, but it's just gotten worse. You would love to be rescued by someone.

You long to hear such words as "I will lead the blind by ways they have not known, along unfamiliar paths I will guide them; I will turn the darkness into light before them and make the rough places smooth. These are the things I will do; I will not forsake them" (Isaiah 42:16, NIV). If any person tells you these things, they will be misleading you, and you will be disappointed again. These words come from God, and he is the only one who can guarantee that they are absolutely true. Ask God to be your guide and protector. He wants to walk with you through your darkness and take you into his light, where he can cure you with his love.

# 122

# Why do people have problems with plurals?

Almost everywhere you go, you will see this mistake. It is printed on signs, added to mailboxes, and sent on envelopes. This error is probably copied time and time again because people assume that if they see it printed, it must be correct. This pervasive problem is how to write the plural of last names.

You're trying to say that there are more members than one in the Robinson, Smith, or Jackson family. Which spelling expresses that? Most people try to add an apostrophe, written as "the Robinson's, the Smith's, or the Jackson's." But this is not correct. No apostrophe is needed. Simply add an *s* to the end of the name (or an *es* if the name already ends in *s* or *x*.) It's that easy. Just remember: "When in doubt, leave the apostrophe out!"

Punctuation marks, spelling rules, correct grammar— they're all just tools we use to help us communicate better. Most of us really want to do a better job when we can, whatever our job may be. We strive to become more efficient, more competent, and more knowledgeable. That's good. The Bible encourages us to work hard and work well. It says, "Whatever your hand finds to do, do it with all your might" (Ecclesiastes 9:10, NIV). Ask God to bless your work and guide your hands.

# Why did the barber need a pole?

The red-and-white pole in front of the barbershop was not just a decoration. It had a meaning for the people who went to the barber during the Middle Ages. At that time barbers did more than cut hair—they served as physicians as well by performing tooth removal and surgery. They even practiced bloodletting, which involved applying leeches to the skin to suck out some blood, supposedly relieving the body of its poisons.

The barber pole tells the story of the bloodletting process. The tools the barber needed were basins to catch the blood and hold the leeches, a pole for the patient to grasp tightly (which made his veins stand out on his arm), and lots of white linen bandages. After this procedure, barbers would hang the cloth strips outside the shop on the gripping pole. Historians disagree on where the red-and-white colors came from.

Some say the bandages were bloody, and the pole was white. Others think that the bandages were washed and hung out to dry on the pole, which was painted red to hide any blood stains. In either case, the strips would spin in the wind and form swirls of red and white. Because not many people in the 1700s could read, the barber pole was an advertisement everyone could understand. In later times, as sanitary conditions improved, the barber pole was merely painted red and white to create the easily recognized symbol. Originally, the leech basin was put on top of the pole, but through the years it came to be represented by the ball.

Barbers used the barber pole to advertise their services. God has his own advertising. The Bible reminds us of this when it says, "The heavens are telling the glory of God; they are a marvelous display of his craftsmanship. Day and night they keep on telling about God. Without a sound or word, silent in the skies, their message reaches out to all the world" (Psalm 19:1-4).

If you were walking past a store that had a display case outside showing a miniature, moving version of the sunrises, sunsets, sparkling stars, and glowing moon, you would be fascinated. You would marvel at how someone could make something so fantastic. You would probably go inside the store, either to see what other amazing things were inside or to buy one of them for yourself. Every day you have access to the gigantic, original version of this display. It's yours for free, to admire and stand in awe of what God can do. God's universe is the best advertising you'll ever see. Tell him today that you want him to use his craftsmanship and power to save your soul. God can make you whole in a way no person, like a barber or a doctor, ever could.

# Why are the sides of a boat called port and starboard?

The right side of a boat is called "starboard." Long ago, Viking ships had a large oar for steering called a steering paddle, or board. It was always attached on the right side because most people are right-handed. This prompted people to call the right side the "steerboard" side. It eventually became the word we use today.

The left side of a ship is called the "port" side. Some people say that's because the big oar on the right side kept boats from pulling up to the land or a dock near the right side. The oar was always in the way. Since the left side of the boat was the side that had to be used when going into port, it became the "port" side. Others say the original word for the left side was "larboard," meaning "empty side."

Although the reason for "port" is unclear, we do know why portholes are round instead of shaped as a normal square or oblong window. It has to do with the stress that is put on a ship from bobbing up and down on the ocean. This motion tends to make the outer covering of the ship "stretch." Corners on the windows would bear the brunt of this stress and might cause the walls of the ship or the glass in the windows to crack. A round window distributes the stress evenly. Also, long ago when the window rims were spun out of bronze or iron on a lathe, circles were naturally easier to shape than a square.

We trust that ships are sturdy enough to keep us afloat. But our safety doesn't depend on metal and wood. The Bible brings this to our attention when it says: "And then there are the sailors sailing the seven seas, plying the trade routes of the world. They, too, observe the power of God in action. He calls to the storm winds; the waves rise high. Their ships are tossed to the heavens and sink again to the depths; the sailors cringe in terror. They reel and stagger like drunkards and are at their wit's end. Then they cry to the Lord in their trouble, and he saves them. He calms the storm and stills the waves. What a blessing is that stillness as he brings them safely into harbor! Oh, that these men would praise the Lord for his loving-kindness and for all of his wonderful deeds!" (Psalm 107:23-31). God surrounds us on all sides, both port and starboard.

# 125

# Which city was named by the toss of a coin?

The only thing they couldn't agree on was a name. Two men were developing a community in Oregon. The property was 640 heavily wooded acres at the mouth of the Willamette River. Amos Lovejoy and Francis Pettygrove were planning the streets and building the first houses in their new city, which still had no name. They finally decided that the only fair thing would be to toss a coin.

Lovejoy wanted the city to be named Boston, in honor of his home state of Massachusetts. He lost the toss. Pettygrove was from Maine, and he wanted to name the city after his state's capital. That's how the Oregon city of Portland got its name.

At some time or another you may have felt like these two developers. You just couldn't decide what to do and figured tossing a coin would give you as good an answer as any other. You may have thought that the results of a coin toss would be impartial and that you were leaving your decision to "chance" or "fate." But God created the world, and he runs it. He is involved in your life as well, and you don't need to feel so alone that a piece of metal can decide what you will do. The Bible tells us, "We toss the coin, but it is the Lord who controls its decision" (Proverbs 16:33). Don't fool with fate. God is the only true source in our life, and through prayer he will guide our every decision.

## 126
# How is Thomas Jefferson connected to the potato chip?

Everyone seemed to enjoy the thick-cut french fries that Thomas Jefferson introduced to America from France in the 1790s. Everyone, that is, except one customer in a restaurant at the Moon Lake Lodge in Saratoga Springs, New York. Native American chef George Crum was losing his patience with this particular customer.

Chef Crum had been sent back to the kitchen with a plate of his thick-cut fries. The critical customer had complained that they weren't thin enough. Another batch was prepared, served, and again rejected. Crum tried one more time but decided to exaggerate. He sliced the potatoes so thinly that they couldn't even be pierced with a fork. Then he soaked them in ice water for a half hour. After he fried and salted them heavily, he presented them to the customer—who loved them! First named "Saratoga chips" in 1835, the treat later became known as "potato chips." Crum was eventually able to open his own restaurant, specializing in—you guessed it—potato chips.

Some people, like Crum's customer, can be a little obsessive and anxious about their food. They inspect it for freshness, fat content, nutritional value, color, and flavor. Although eating is an enjoyable part of life, it, like anything else, can sometimes distract you from what's really important. If you study the menu longer than you study the Bible, there's something you should know. Jesus says, "Man does not live on bread alone, but on every word that comes from the mouth of God" (Matthew 4:4, NIV). Fill your soul first, your stomach afterward, and you will feel better about both.

# Why are detectives called private eyes?

Allan Pinkerton made spying his business. The first case he cracked involved a counterfeiting ring. At the time he wasn't even a detective, but he decided he could make a living at it. In 1850 he started the Pinkerton National Detective Agency. He taught America to call detectives "private investigators" or "private i's" for short.

To go along with the term *private i,* Pinkerton used a wide-open eye as the logo for his company, along with the slogan, "We Never Sleep." After a while detectives became known as "private eyes." Pinkerton went on to become President Lincoln's bodyguard and to serve as head of the Secret Service during the Civil War.

When something really piques your interest, you tend to be more alert than when you're bored. The ever-open eye of the Pinkerton Detective Agency suggested that he would always be curious about what you were doing—enough to keep him awake at night. The Bible talks about the anxiousness of waiting for something special or important when it says, "My soul waits for the Lord more than watchmen wait for the morning" (Psalm 130:6, NIV). It is that excitement, yearning, and attention that pleases God. If you are always aware that God is nearby, you won't miss the blessings he wants to give you.

# 128

## Who was Charles Boycott?

Charles Boycott didn't know that his name would one day go down in history when he took a job as a landlord's agent in Ireland. In 1879, when poor harvests threatened the economy, a workers' group, similar to a labor union of today, insisted on lower rents for the tenant farmers. Boycott responded by attempting to serve notices of eviction to the tenants in his jurisdiction. The tenants, acting on the advice of the workers' group, refused not only to leave their homes but to work. As a result, Boycott lost his job, left town, and left his name to be a part of protests of all kinds from that time forward.

Your attitude has a lot to do with what people think of you. If Charles Boycott hadn't been excessively ruthless, his name probably wouldn't have been associated with such a negative event. If he had followed the example of Jesus, treating those people kindly and with compassion, and possibly helping them find alternatives to make their rent hike less painful, he wouldn't have left a "bad guy" legacy.

Think carefully about your actions. Try as hard as you can to keep your name linked with words like *right, good, decency,* and *respect*. The Bible sums it up: "A good name is better than fine perfume" (Ecclesiastes 7:1, NIV). Keep the atmosphere around you as sweet and inviting as you can, and you will be amazed at the rewards that come to you because of your attractive reputation.

# What kind of puzzle took five years to solve?

Workers building a new road near one of the great Pyramids in 1954 uncovered something unusual. Under a hill of sand, they found many stone blocks. Under those blocks, there was a "box" carved into the limestone. In the box were 1,224 pieces of wood, lots of rope, and some reed mats. The wood pieces were stacked in 13 layers. What had the workers discovered?

Ahmed Youssef, an Egyptian master restorer, had the answer. Each piece of wood had a hieroglyphic on it that described where it belonged. The oldest puzzle in the world was waiting to be reassembled! Ahmed spent a year and a half taking the wood out of the box and restoring the rotted or bent pieces. It took four more years to put all the pieces in order because only ropes or pegs held them together. Finally, a wooden picture of a funeral barge, or boat, became apparent. The more-than-4,000-year-old puzzle had finally been solved.

Making your way toward heaven is similar to waiting for Ahmed's puzzle to be solved. You know the end will be great, and you're excited about seeing it for the first time. But you know you have to wait patiently. Ahmed was rewarded with a completed puzzle. God will reward you for not giving up on your quest to do his will. The Bible says, "He will give each one whatever his deeds deserve. He will give eternal life to those who patiently do the will of God, seeking for the unseen glory and honor and eternal life that he offers" (Romans 2:6-7). Dig into the Bible, and you'll find all the pieces you need for your journey toward heaven.

# 130
# What is the dollar bill saying with symbols?

Seen a dollar bill lately? Did you notice all the symbolism? If not, you might want to take a second look. It may seem strange that an American bill would have a pyramid on it, but it's there in the middle of a circle. The pyramid is supposed to symbolize the strength and permanence of our country. Look closely, and you'll notice that the pyramid is unfinished. It means that America looks forward to growth and perfection in the future. There's also an eye near the top of the pyramid. That's the overseeing, all-seeing eye of God.

*Annuit Coeptis* is a Latin reference to God meaning "He has favored our undertakings." At the bottom of the circle are the words *Novus Ordo Seclorum,* also Latin, meaning "A new order of the ages" and intended to show hope for the new American era. Finally, there's the Roman numeral MDCCLXXVI inscribed on the base of the pyramid. In case you're a little rusty, that means 1776—the beginning of the "new era" of America's independence from England.

The other circle is just as interesting. The eagle holds an olive branch that has 13 leaves and 13 berries, standing for the original 13 colonies. In the other claw are 13 arrows. The olive branch means peace; the arrows mean war; and the eagle's head is turned toward one and away from the other, indicating early America's hopes for peace.

The designers of the dollar bill had obviously read their Bible. It says, "The eyes of the Lord are in every place, keeping watch on the evil and the good" (Proverbs 15:3, RSV). When you were a child, it reassured you to know that your parents were watching out for you. They stood between you and a world that was sometimes frightening. Then you grew up and eventually realized that you had grown beyond their ability to protect you.

If you sometimes miss the feeling of being sheltered and guided, and if you're wishing you had just one person who was always on your side, it might be time for you to strengthen your relationship with God. He sees everything—your pain, doubts, and fears. He wants to accompany you through your future. He is absolutely trustworthy and absolutely willing to be your comfort and stronghold. He will nurture and love you in a way even your parents couldn't or didn't do. You can go back to the joys of childhood by committing to be God's child. Turn your burdens and responsibilities over to him, and he will bear them with you, and even for you.

# How did an ocean liner get the wrong name?

Sir Thomas Royden didn't choose his words carefully enough in 1934. Sir Thomas was the director of the British Cunard transatlantic ocean liners. A new ship was almost ready to be launched. It just needed a name. Sir Thomas had decided that the new vessel should be christened as the *Queen Victoria*, but he needed the king's permission first.

King George V received a visit from Sir Thomas, who asked the king if the new ocean liner could be named "after the greatest queen this country has ever known." King George loved the idea and, referring to his wife, Mary, replied, "That is the greatest compliment ever paid to my wife. I'll ask her." Sir Thomas knew right then that he should never mention his original idea and that he would be christening the new ship as the *Queen Mary*.

Sir Thomas knew that he had made a mistake in choosing his words. He was probably relieved that his error wasn't discovered. Maybe something like this has happened to you before: Either you got away from an embarrassing moment without being exposed, or you made your mistake around someone who was understanding and compassionate and didn't hold it against you. It's a great feeling of relief to realize you won't be penalized in the way that you know you deserve.

That's how you'll feel when you accept Jesus into your heart. The all-powerful, almighty exalted Lord could justifiably crush you in an instant for all the sins you've committed. Some people might try to convince you that God is vengeful, angry, and vindictive. But the Bible tells a different story. It says, "For the Son of man is not come to destroy men's lives, but to save them" (Luke 9:56, KJV). Accept forgiveness and compassion. Be released from guilt. Then accept the invitation to begin again with God.

## 132

# How did the question mark get its strange shape?

The question mark is one of the most strangely shaped punctuation marks. Who decided what it would look like and why? The story of the question mark starts back in the time when Latin was the standard language. After each question, the Latin word *questio* (question) was written. That was a lot of work.

As an alternative, people started using the abbreviation QO at the end of every question. The problem with that idea was that the reader would often think the QO was part of the spelling of the last word. This was very confusing. Soon people began writing the Q above the O, lined up like a mathematical fraction. As time passed, the shape of the Q became more and more eroded, and the O turned into a simple dot. The result of these changes was the question mark as we know it today.

Asking questions is how we learn. The most important question you'll ever ask is, "How can I make my life count?" The Bible tells you how to find out. It says, "If you want to know what God wants you to do, ask him, and he will gladly tell you, for he is always ready to give a bountiful supply of wisdom to all who ask him; he will not resent it" (James 1:5). Every question that you ask God is a good one because he is the ultimate authority for every answer.

## 133

# Why did the rainmaker lose his job?

How do you know when you've had too much of a good thing? The city of San Diego found out the hard way in 1915. That was the year that Charles Hatfield offered the city council the chance to fill up the nearby reservoir, which had never been more than one-third full since it was created. Hatfield considered himself to be a rainmaker, and he gave the city a special offer.

If he caused rain, the city would pay him $10,000; if no rain came, no payment would be expected. The council agreed that they had nothing to lose and hired Hatfield. He built a 20-foot tower near the reservoir and put some of his specially mixed chemicals on the top. Four days later it began to rain. Five days after that, steady rain was falling over the whole county, and it lasted for 10 more days.

So much rain fell that the water rushed through downtown San Diego, stopping business. Rivers overflowed; telephone and telegraph services stopped working; railroads and roads were shut down. Buildings were swept away. Then the sun came out—just long enough for people to begin repairs—but then another downpour started. After filling up the reservoir at a pace of two feet every hour, the rain finally stopped when the reservoir was only five inches away from overflowing.

The long-term effects were that the trains didn't run for at least a month, more than 200 bridges were ruined, and, worst of all, 50 people died. Hatfield felt that he had kept his bargain and was shocked when the city council said he would not be paid unless he could prove that he had been the cause of the rain. That was basically impossible to prove, so Hatfield never got paid.

Could rainmaking be scientifically done at that time? Not really. In earlier days, people thought that explosions could cause rain because they often noticed a downpour after a battle. In the 1880s one con-man would send up a hot-air balloon to fire artillery into the sky, just before an obvious rainstorm was coming. But it was only after the mid-1940s that "seeding" was developed. A pilot sprays fluffy cumulus clouds, which are the only ones that will respond, with powdered dry ice or carbon dioxide. As moisture collects around these particles, they become too heavy to stay in the clouds, and the liquid falls as rain or snow.

When the ground is dry, rain is very exciting. God understands this feeling and uses rain to explain about his blessings. He says, "I will make my people and their homes around my hill a blessing. And there shall be showers, showers of blessing, for I will not shut off the rains but send them in their seasons" (Ezekiel 34:26). Turn your face up toward heaven and let God's blessings pour over you.

## 134

# What legacy did Henrietta Lacks leave?

Great medical strides have been made in the diagnosis and treatment of cancer, but in 1951, when Henrietta Lacks was found to have cervical cancer, not much was known. Eight months after her diagnosis, even with treatment, Henrietta died at the age of 31. But part of Henrietta lives on because her cancerous cells have been of invaluable help to scientists.

A doctor at Henrietta's hospital noticed that samples of her cells multiplied extremely quickly. He sent some of the cells to a biologist who specialized in tissue culture at Johns Hopkins University. Tissue culture involves cultivating cells in a controlled environment so that they can be studied and tested. Most cells die when removed from the body, but Henrietta's cells kept reproducing.

They were named HeLa cells, after the first two letters of each of her names, and the cells have been helpful in many areas of research. In fact, the HeLa cells were used to help find the cure for polio. For the first time, scientists could study cells grown in laboratory conditions rather than in animals. HeLa cells have also been used in genetic engineering research, vaccine development, and cancer studies. Henrietta shared her cells with doctors, doctors have shared them with each other, and the medical community has shared the resulting research with the world.

We should be very grateful for the legacy Henrietta left behind because she made it possible for us to learn how to prolong our life on earth. But when you belong to God's family, you will receive an even greater heritage. The Bible says, "God has reserved for his children the priceless gift of eternal life; it is kept in heaven for you, pure and undefiled, beyond the reach of change and decay" (1 Peter 1:4). No matter how valuable, nothing that man leaves behind will last forever. Only this inheritance from God will be permanent. Have you prepared your heirs to receive God's inheritance? It's the most valuable testament you can ever leave behind.

## 135
# Which was worse—a snowstorm or a private meeting with the president?

It was the heaviest snowstorm in 10 years, and David Marston had to travel in it. He was the United States attorney for Pennsylvania, and his ultimate boss, the presi-

dent of the United States, wanted him in Washington, D.C.,
immediately.

First Marston tried the airlines, but no flights were able to
depart. Driving a car was impossible. That left trains. In Phil-
adelphia, Marston boarded the train, but he only got as far
as Baltimore because the train became stuck when it
derailed. Next, Marston found a bus headed for Washington, D. C., and that was how he completed his trip to his
office in the Capitol. When Marston finally arrived, he
found out why the president had asked him to come. Marston was being fired, and President Carter thought it would
be kinder if he heard the news in person.

Marston went to great trouble to perform his duty for the
president, and he didn't even receive a reward. Maybe that's
happened to you. You worked really hard on a project, and
then someone else got the credit; the promotion you
deserved went to someone else; despite all the years you
gave to the company, you were laid off. How can you
handle disappointments like these?

First of all, realize that you're not responsible to an
earthly person—your boss is really God, and you'll never
lose your job as his ambassador. The Bible offers a different
perspective for keeping the big picture in mind. It says, "We
can rejoice, too, when we run into problems and trials, for
we know that they are good for us—they help us learn to be
patient. And patience develops strength of character in us
and helps us trust God more each time we use it until
finally our hope and faith are strong and steady. Then, when
that happens, we are able to hold our heads high no matter
what happens and know that all is well, for we know how

dearly God loves us" (Romans 5:3-5). Cling to God in times of trouble, and he will carry you through.

─────────────────────────── **136**

# How was a wedding ring reclaimed after it was lost at sea?

Prince Urussof was a worried newlywed. He and his bride were on their honeymoon, sailing on the Black Sea. The prince was remembering a family story passed down to him about wedding rings. The belief was that if you lost the ring, you lost the bride. That's what was troubling him—his bride's ring had just slipped off her finger and fallen into the sea. How could he get it back?

Although he tried to think of a way to retrieve the ring, it seemed impossible. So he settled for the next best thing. He went up and down both shores of the Black Sea, buying the properties that touched the shores. The prince spent $40 million making deals with hundreds of owners. Now he "owned" the Black Sea and everything in it—including the wedding ring at the bottom. After the prince's death, his descendants no longer needed the ring, so they sold the Black Sea properties for $80 million, a 100 percent profit.

The prince spent lots of money and effort trying to "recover" the lost wedding ring. It makes a charming tale because we all like to think that love is so strong that someone will go to the ends of the earth to preserve it. But there is a much more powerful love story that involves each one of us. When you die, your body will be covered with earth, just as the ring was covered by water. The valuable part of your body—your soul, which could easily have been counted "lost"—will be raised to heaven through the death of Jesus, who paid the highest price—his very life—to regain your soul. The Bible says, "God will redeem my life from the grave; he will surely take me to himself" (Psalm 49:15, NIV).

## 137
# Where does the asphalt go from a pothole?

Let's talk road maintenance. We've all seen those rubber reflectors that are imbedded in the road. They were invented in 1934 to help drivers stay on course at night, and they're referred to as "cat's eyes." Inside the rubber casing is yellow-colored glass that attracts the light coming from a car's headlights. Cat's eyes are basically maintenance-free for two reasons. First, the rubber case is used to protect the glass from cracking when a tire rolls over it. Second, the cat's eyes are designed to be "self-cleaning." The pressure of a tire pushes the rubber case against the glass eye, and the rubber moves across the glass, wiping it clean.

Potholes, however, can't take care of themselves. They're caused mainly by moisture that is absorbed by the concrete. Add to that the freeze-thaw cycle, traffic wear, and chemicals, and soon the pavement crumbles from within. It's easy to figure out how potholes are filled up, but how are potholes emptied out? In other words, where does all the asphalt that used to be in the potholes go? It's a combination of conditions that removes the broken asphalt. Vehicle tires scatter it, rain carries it away, and wind pushes it onto the road shoulders.

And what about those manholes? Why are the covers round, instead of square or oblong? No matter which way it's turned, the round manhole cover can't fall through the hole; it's kept in place by a lip rimming the inside of the hole.

As you travel on patched and potholed roads, don't let yourself be dragged down into the muck and mire. Instead, keep this glimpse of the road to heaven in your head: "And a main road will go through that once-deserted land; it will be named 'The Holy Highway.' No evil-hearted men may walk upon it. God will walk there with you; even the most stupid cannot miss the way. No lion will lurk along its course, nor will there be any other dangers; only the redeemed will travel there. These, the ransomed of the Lord, will go home along that road to Zion, singing the songs of everlasting joy. For them all sorrow and all sighing will be gone forever; only joy and gladness will be there" (Isaiah 35:8-10). Point your heart toward Jesus and travel on with confidence!

# 138

# Why was a bank alarmed about a withdrawal?

Imagine yourself taking an ordinary trip to the bank, intending to withdraw $50. You take a slip from the stack, fill it out, and hand it to the teller. The next thing you know, you're in big trouble. The police have been called by secret alarm, and the person they want to arrest is you! That's what happened to Ron Schatz of Rhode Island.

He had no idea what he had done wrong. It took a while to straighten out the story. The teller had pressed the silent alarm after turning over Ron's withdrawal slip and seeing the words "This is a holdup" on the back. She had no way of knowing that Ron hadn't written the message. It was discovered that the whole stack of withdrawal slips had the same words printed on the back—someone's idea of a practical joke.

Look at the chain reaction just a few words on paper can cause! The actions of Jesus and the news of his sacrifice can have a much more startling effect. They can change your whole life. The Bible tells us, "It was through what his Son did that God cleared a path for everything to come to him— all things in heaven and on earth—for Christ's death on the cross has made peace with God for all by his blood. This includes you who were once so far away from God. You were his enemies and hated him and were separated from him by your evil thoughts and actions, yet now he has brought you back as his friends. He has done this through the death on the cross of his own human body, and now as a result Christ has brought you into the very presence of God, and you are standing there before him with nothing left against you—nothing left that he could even chide you for; the only condition is that you fully believe the Truth, standing in it steadfast and firm, strong in the Lord, convinced of the Good News that Jesus died for you, and never shifting from trusting him to save you. This is the wonderful news that came to each of you and is now spreading all over the world" (Colossians 1:20-23). Act as quickly on reading the words above as the teller did when she read the note. The stakes are much higher than just protecting money—you will be moving to save your soul for all eternity.

## 139

# How do rocks travel in Death Valley?

Death Valley is a place of extremes because it is the driest, hottest, and lowest location in America. Something extremely odd happens there, too. There is a three-mile-long, dried-up lakebed in Death Valley, and all across it, rocks and stones leave small paths behind them in curved, zigzagged, or straight patterns. The rocks aren't alive, of course, yet they travel across the lakebed. How?

Dr. Robert Sharp, a geology professor, decided to find out about the roaming rocks. He put tags on 30 stones of different sizes and shapes. He hammered spikes into the ground where the rocks were sitting, and then he studied what happened for the next seven years. Twenty-eight of the stones did indeed move, sometimes more than 600 feet. Sharp matched the movements of the rocks with the weather conditions and found that the rocks moved due to wind and rain. Even though Death Valley gets less than two inches of rain a year, the raindrops make the smooth clay in the lakebed very slick. The wind then blows the rocks across the slippery surface, sometimes as fast as three feet per second.

The sight of these "moving rocks" is amazing because we're used to the fact that rocks stay put and do not move on their own. That's precisely why a big rock was put in front of Jesus' tomb when he died. It was even guarded, to keep the disciples from pushing it away. The rock was supposed to be proof that Jesus didn't rise from the dead. But God keeps his promises. The Bible says, "Suddenly there was a great earthquake; for an angel of the Lord came down from heaven and rolled aside the stone and sat on it" (Matthew 28:2). Desert rocks that move on their own are fascinating, but an angel perched on a dislodged rock is a true miracle!

## 140
# How did a fire alarm improve baking bread?

If not for an unexpected fire alarm, you might not be able to enjoy fresh-baked rolls with your meals at home. Almost everyone appreciates the smell and taste of this type of bread, but very few people have the extra hours needed to mix, knead, and let the dough rise.

That was Joe Gregor's problem. He had spent many hours experimenting, trying to figure out how to shorten the time needed to bake rolls. He was having no success. Joe, a volunteer fireman in Florida, was baking another batch of rolls when the fire siren screeched. Joe quickly pulled the rolls out of the oven, dumped them on the counter, and raced for the fire. When he returned, he inspected the white, cold, plastery dough. Rather than throwing it away, Joe decided to reheat the oven and finish baking his bread. To his surprise, the rolls turned out perfectly. After experimenting a little more to determine the exact times and temperatures, Joe spread the word about how bakers could do all the preliminary work leaving the last, best part for their customers.

We often wonder if God will answer our prayers. Sometimes we are suspicious of such unconditional love because it's so hard for us to love that way. Jesus understands our doubts and impatience. He's also aware of our fondness for bread. That's why he gives us reassurance in this way: "If a child asks his father for a loaf of bread, will he be given a stone instead? If he asks for fish, will he be given a poisonous snake? Of course not! And if you hard-hearted, sinful men know how to give good gifts to your children, won't your Father in heaven even more certainly give good gifts to those who ask him for them?" (Matthew 7:9-11). God holds the perfect recipe for our life, and his timing is never wrong. He hears our prayers more quickly and answers them more abundantly than an entire oven full of quick-bake rolls.

# 141

## How do seeds always know to send their roots downward?

When you are planting, there's no way to figure out which side of the seed will be growing the roots. You just plop the seed in and cover it up. Yet you never see a plant pushing its roots toward the sun and its leaves into the ground. How does it happen that the plant always grows right-side-up?

In the ground, the seed first sends out a root. Then it sends out a stem shaped like a hook. The root points down, the stem points up. Scientists call the root development "positive geotropism" and the stem growth "negative geotropism." When the stem breaks through the earth and starts to grow toward the sun, its "hook" straightens out, and that's called "phototropism." (Phototropism, by the way, is why a plant always turns toward the sun. Plants develop more cells on the darker side of their stems. The dark side grows faster, and the plant tilts toward its "sunny" side).

The growth from a seed always happens in the same order, in the same way. The secret to the seed has a much simpler name than its scientific label. It's called gravity. The root pushes toward the center of the earth, moving with the pull of gravity. The stem pushes away from the pull of gravity, toward the earth's surface. That's why you don't see any upside-down gardens. On earth, seeds are always predictable. It's only in outer space, where there is no gravity, that seeds have no clue how to grow. There, a seed will grow in any direction.

The root grows in the right direction for the plant to survive. We need to grow toward God so that our souls can survive. The Bible says, "May your roots go down deep into the soil of God's marvelous love; and may you be able to feel and understand, as all God's children should, how long, how wide, how deep, and how high his love really is; and to experience this love for yourselves, though it is so great that you will never see the end of it or fully know or understand it. And so at last you will be filled up with God himself" (Ephesians 3:17-19). All of God's children gathered together will make a gorgeous garden!

## 142

# How did restaurants start from the French Revolution?

When you're trying to decide which restaurant to go to, you can thank the French Revolution for giving you a choice. What do a war and a restaurant have to do with each other? Before the Revolution, you could eat away from home, but the taverns served only one dish at a certain time. You could also go to a cookshop, where they would give you already-cooked meat to take home for a meal.

Along came a Frenchman named Boulanger, who sold soups. He put a sign outside his shop saying Restoratives, meaning that you could get your strength or health back if you consumed his hot broths. What the sign said in French was *Restaurant*. Boulanger offered several different kinds of soups, which made his the first eating place to offer a menu.

It was the French Revolution, however, that changed the concept of "eating out" forever. Prior to the Revolution, all the wealthy French aristocrats had highly talented cooks working for them. After the war, aristocrats were stripped of their wealth, leaving lots of cooks unemployed. These chefs joined the staff of existing restaurants or opened up their own until there were more than 500 restaurants in France by 1804.

We are free to choose whatever pleases us in a restaurant. We are also free to choose whether we will follow God. Moses said, "Today I have set before you life or death, blessing or curse. Oh, that you would choose life; that you and your children might live! Choose to love the Lord your God and to obey him and to cling to him, for he is your life and the length of your days" (Deuteronomy 30:19-20). You could search for the rest of your life, but you'll never find a better deal on any other menu.

# Why is the ocean so salty?

Seawater collects its salt by starting in rivers, which flow against land along the way and pull minerals from the ground. Rain falling on the land washes more minerals into the rivers. Rivers also rush across rocks, washing even more minerals downstream into the ocean.

But not all bodies of water have the same amount of salt. If the seawater has a river near its shore, the water will be less salty because it is diluted by the fresh river water. If the seawater is shallow, it will be more salty due to evaporation. When the sun dries up water, the water leaves its salt deposits behind. The Dead Sea, for example, experiences lots of evaporation because it is surrounded by a dry desert.

The Dead Sea contains so much salt—about 25 percent—that it is virtually impossible to drown in its water. The salt makes the water "heavy," which makes the swimmer's body buoyant enough to stay near the surface. Average seawater has only about 3½ percent salt, but it is still easier to stay afloat in seawater than in a freshwater lake or pool. Why is rain not salty when it falls if it is collected from salty water? The salt is too heavy to rise with the water vapor as it evaporates from the ocean.

In the same way that salt can keep you floating above danger in the water, God can keep you floating above danger in life. Just ask him to help you by saying, "Hold me safe above the heads of all my enemies; then I can continue to obey your laws" (Psalm 119:117). When someone rescues you, you want to reciprocate by doing something extra in return. Your loyalty to God will please him greatly.

# 144
# What is the history of the sandwich?

He was right in the middle of a card game when his servants brought the meal. John Montague had asked that his roast be placed between two slices of toast and handed to him at the table. That way he could eat and play at the same time. Montague did this so often that his friends began naming this special meal after him. Of course, Montague didn't invent the sandwich.

As early as Roman times, people were putting food between pieces of bread; the Romans called it *offula*. Montague just made the sandwich more popular. His birthday, November 3, is considered "Sandwich Day." Before the Hawaiian Islands had their names changed, they were called the Sandwich Islands because the discoverer, Captain James Cook, named them after Montague. How do we know all of this? Because John Montague was the earl of Sandwich. Now there are so many varieties of sandwiches, they have their own names, like "heroes," "poor boys," "hoagies," and "submarines."

The earl of Sandwich was so involved in what he was doing, he didn't even want to take time to eat. Maybe you're feeling that's the story of your life, too. You're working day and night, trying to keep everything together. There's definitely no extra time for fun or relaxation—there's not even enough time to fulfill all of your responsibilities. Maybe you're not spending time with your family, but you're doing all you can to support them. You're afraid that if you don't keep up and stay competitive, you'll lose your edge. Your days are just a succession of tasks to be accomplished. You'd like things to be different, but you don't know how to change them. It might surprise you to know that God understands. He knows what being harassed, harried, and overwhelmed feels like. God has a special invitation just for you.

He says, "Come to me and I will give you rest—all of you who work so hard beneath a heavy yoke" (Matthew 11:28). When's the last time you got an offer of help from someone who really had the power to change things? Test God and see for yourself. Steal a few minutes out of your schedule each day to talk to him. Tell him how hard it is. You will begin to feel more rested because God will give you wisdom. He will change your perspective and help you identify your priorities. He will refresh you with the reminder that you're not alone—he is your backup and will never let you down. As you begin to trust God more and more, he will give more strength to you. You will begin to see ways to make better use of your time; things will become clearer. Slow down and let him feed you with his comfort and reassurance. That will be one meal worth savoring.

# 145

## Why is it impossible to buy fresh sardines?

Have you ever tried asking for fresh sardines at the supermarket seafood counter? If not, save yourself the embarrassment. They won't have any. That's because there is no such fish as a sardine. Yes, you can buy a can labeled sardines, but that name only applies to the fish after they're in the tin. Sardine cans are really packed with any one of 21 species of small fish. Every country is allowed to define what kind of fish its "sardines" will be.

Each country sends fishermen out to catch the small fish that will be sold as sardines. Jesus used the job of fishing to show how much more important our work can be when we work for him. He said, "Come along with me and I will show you how to fish for the souls of men!" (Matthew 4:19). Instead of bringing in a fish for canning, imagine the satisfaction of helping a soul to reach heaven.

# How do you return the favor of a rescue?

It only took an instant. Four-year-old Roger Lausier was playing in the beach sand, and then he vanished. He had waded into the ocean and stepped off a ledge into deeper water over his head. When he opened his mouth to yell, the water began to choke him. At that instant someone grabbed him and pulled him up. Alice Blaise saved Roger's life after seeing the boy disappear—something his parents had missed by being distracted for just one moment. Roger's parents were grateful to Alice because they got their son back.

The family continued to vacation at that same beach near Salem, Massachusetts. By the age of 13, Roger was a very good swimmer. One day that summer Roger noticed a man out in the ocean who was struggling and yelling for help. Roger took his air raft and floated it beside him as he swam to reach the man. With Roger's help, the man was able to lay across the raft and be towed to shore. Only after the rescue did Roger find out the identity of the man: He was Alice Blaise's husband.

When Alice pulled little Roger from the waves, she didn't know her actions would be reciprocated in the rescuing of her husband several years later. But that's how God works. He promises, "If you give, you will get! Your gift will return to you in full and overflowing measure, pressed down, shaken together to make room for more, and running over. Whatever measure you use to give—large or small—will be used to measure what is given back to you" (Luke 6:38). Alice wasn't thinking about helping herself nine years earlier as she bravely saved young Roger. God kept his word in an unusual way as he blessed Alice for her gift to Roger. She received the precious life of her husband.

## 147

# Why don't birds seem frightened by scarecrows?

It's not unusual to see a scarecrow with birds perched along its arms. You have to wonder why the farmers go to all that trouble if the crows aren't even afraid. Some scarecrows were first made because the farmers were scared. They worried about evil spirits. They thought they could protect their crops from any damage by putting two branches together in the shape of a cross and sticking the cross into the ground. Then, to camouflage the cross, they hung old clothes over it.

Other farmers used scarecrows because they really were having trouble with the birds. It was so bad that they planted four seeds in each hole—two for the birds, one for the worms, and one to grow. Native Americans sometimes assigned a real man to stand in the middle of their fields, waving and throwing rocks. That's probably where they got the idea to make a scarecrow that looked like a person. The scarecrows actually did keep those pesky crows away for a while.

It wasn't the way the scarecrow looked that bothered the birds, though. The scent of humans clung to the newly hung clothes and kept the crows out of the fields. But after wind, rain, and fresh air swept the scent away, the birds saw that the scarecrow never moved and weren't scared anymore.

Anything that man makes won't offer permanent protection. No law, weapon, or barrier lasts forever. Only God's defense of your soul can be counted on to remain constant throughout eternity. The Bible says, "For your kingdom never ends. You rule generation after generation" (Psalm 145:13). If you're concerned about the well-being of your family, your descendants, and yourself, protect your precious crop with the love of Jesus.

## 148

# Why was telling time tricky on trains?

Because one man had a better idea, all of us have less scheduling headaches. If we had lived in 1882, managing our time would have been infinitely more complicated. The problem was that the United States was divided into too many different time zones. There were more than 80 "correct" times across the country.

Whenever the sun was directly overhead, it was presumed to be noon. If it was 12:00 p.m. in Massachusetts, it was only 10:49 a.m. in Georgia. Trying to arrange a train trip from one end of the country to the other was practically impossible since each railroad company used its own idea of what time it was supposed to be. As the ability to travel longer distances grew, people began to realize that the time zones needed to be changed—otherwise a passenger would need to adjust the hands on his watch 20 times on a coast-to-coast trip.

The hero of this story was Charles F. Dowd. In 1869 he published a plan for dividing the United States into only four time zones, varying four hours across the country, based on the time in Washington, D.C. Later, it was decided that Greenwich, England, should be the standard that would be used for these zones. This standardization of time was expanded worldwide, and by 1918 it became law.

We often think that if we could just master the time, we would be in control of our life. But we are so powerless that we can't even influence a simple thing like the arrival of a train or plane. If it doesn't come when it's supposed to, we can't do anything about it but adjust and adapt. Jesus, on the other hand, is unfailingly in complete control. The Bible reminds us, "He was before all else began and it is his power that holds everything together" (Colossians 1:17). While we are striving just to keep up with our appointments, Jesus is effortlessly scheduling the whole world.

# When were dirty tennis shoes helpful?

A dirty tennis shoe is responsible for keeping your couch cleaner. The owner of the shoes was wearing them one day when she was in the research lab at the 3M company. The 3M researchers were experimenting with some chemicals they planned to use on aircraft. Some of the chemical spilled onto her tennis shoe, and it wouldn't come off. No matter how dirty the shoe got, the spot where the chemical had dropped stayed clean. That's how the fluorochemical became noticed, and that's how Scotchgard was invented. Scotchgard coats material, repels stains, and helps furniture stay cleaner and last longer.

If your sneakers are Scotchgarded, you feel freer to walk around. You're not worried about damaging them beyond repair. As God's children, we have "Scotchgard" for our heart as well as our feet. In a very special way, God protects us from being soiled or damaged. The Bible says, "He orders his angels to protect you wherever you go. They will steady you with their hands to keep you from stumbling against the rocks on the trail. You can safely meet a lion or step on poisonous snakes, yes, even trample them beneath your feet!" (Psalm 91:11-13). Only God's power can protect our steps and keep us spotless!

# 150
# What's the best way to clean?

There are a few things you should know about cleansers. Anything that is advertised as a scourer, even a "soft" one, will eventually scratch porcelain, even if you just rub lightly each time. Always start with a soft cloth or sponge, using something rougher only if necessary. When using chlorine bleach, don't mix in any other type of cleanser. Chlorine reacts with other chemicals and produces a dangerous gas. And cover your jewelry or remove it completely while cleaning. Some cleansers can damage gems by scratching, dulling, or discoloring the polished surfaces.

If you had the opportunity, wouldn't you love to turn all your cleaning chores over to someone else? The bad news is that most of us will probably have to do much of the housecleaning ourselves. The good news is that we can have a sparkling clean, pure soul, and we don't need to worry about which cleansers will work. We can't do it alone, though. God will be happy to change the condition of our soul by wiping away all the dirt inside. Say to him, "Though sins fill our hearts, you forgive them all" (Psalm 65:3). When you acknowledge and ask for God's power, you will have access to his service. Cleaning can't get much easier or be more important than that.

# How was the peace sign developed?

No matter how you felt about it at the time, there is one object from our past that was so distinctive, almost everyone, young or old, can still identify it. Yet how it was developed is not widely known. The object is the peace symbol—that circle with the lines inside it.

The shape and placement of those lines were actually significant in the peace symbol. The lines stood for letters. The letters were *N* and *D*. If you never saw the letters in the design, it's because they weren't placed there to look like letters. The lines were created from the flag (or semaphore) signals for the letters *N* and *D*, which stood for "nuclear disarmament." Bertrand Russell introduced the peace symbol in 1958, after it was designed by the Direct Action Committee.

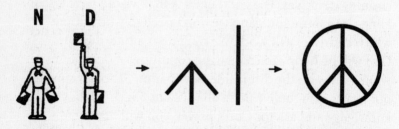

People can't offer peace to others if they haven't yet found it within themselves. If peace only comes one by one, where do you start? With yourself, of course. And where can you find peace? In Jesus Christ. He promises, "I am leaving you with a gift—peace of mind and heart! And the peace I give isn't fragile like the peace the world gives. So don't be troubled or afraid" (John 14:27). To experience peace, don't wait on the world—wait on the Lord.

## 152

# What were the shortest letters ever written?

Authors are sometimes known to be wordy, but no one can accuse Victor Hugo of that fault. He had just written his novel *Les Miserables,* and he was curious about how well it was selling. Hugo sent a message to his publisher. The entire note said, "?" The publisher replied in kind. His answer was simply, "!"

Compared to eternity, our life on earth is as short as Victor Hugo's letter. The Bible says, "Lord, through all the generations you have been our home! Before the mountains were created, before the earth was formed, you are God without beginning or end. You speak, and man turns back to dust. A thousand years are but as yesterday to you! They are like a single hour! We glide along the tides of time as swiftly as a racing river and vanish as quickly as a dream. We are like grass that is green in the morning but mowed down and withered before the evening shadows fall. . . . Teach us to number our days and recognize how few they are; help us to spend them as we should" (Psalm 90:1-6,12). Spend as much time as you can making sure that your soul is guaranteed life everlasting.

---

# 153

# What does it mean to give someone the cold shoulder?

When we are given the cold shoulder, we are ignored or snubbed and not welcomed warmly. It's almost as if someone is turning his back on us. But the "shoulder" referred to in this saying does not mean a person's shoulder. It stands for the shoulder of an animal.

During the Middle Ages, the shoulder was the least-desirable cut from an animal that would be cooked. It would be the most likely piece to be a leftover. When poor people would beg for a meal, they would be given a shoulder that hadn't even been warmed up. On occasion even the nobility would receive this meal. If you were visiting someone's castle, and he felt that you had stayed long enough, he might have a cold shoulder of mutton served to you, as a hint that he was tired of treating you royally.

The Bible has a very straightforward comment on this subject. It advises, "Don't visit your neighbor too often, or you will outwear your welcome!" (Proverbs 25:17). People aren't perfect. They're not as patient or generous or concerned as we would like for them to be. If you're looking for all these qualities in a friend or neighbor, you're looking in the wrong place. God is the one who will never grow tired of spending time with you. He invites you to enjoy his company and encourages you to stay forever. Nurture your friendship with God by talking to him in prayer all the time. The more often you visit him through prayer, the more welcome you'll be in his house.

## 154

# How did sideburns get their name?

The name for that extra hair growing in front of men's ears has gotten tangled up through time. You may think that the *side* in *sideburns* comes from the fact that the hair is located on each side of a man's face. But that leaves no explanation for the second half of the word, *burns*.

The real reason we use the word *sideburns* is because during the Civil War, there was a general who was fond of wearing his hair this way. His name was Ambrose E. Burnside. Somehow through the years his name was turned around, but he is the gentleman credited with starting the fashion all the same.

We imitate fashion trends to show that we admire a certain style or identify with a certain group. Copying fads is amusing, but it is a fairly superficial way of "belonging." The Bible encourages us to be much more serious when choosing a whole lifestyle. We are to look beyond the present and calculate what will be happening in the future.

The Bible explains, "Knowing what lies ahead for you, you won't become bored with being a Christian nor become spiritually dull and indifferent, but you will be anxious to follow the example of those who receive all that God has promised them because of their strong faith and patience" (Hebrews 6:12). Enjoy experimenting with and changing your "outside," but make sure that your "inside" is securely anchored to God.

## 155

# How did a broken church organ inspire the creation of a carol?

The church organ was broken, the repairman couldn't come, and the Christmas Eve services needed some music that didn't yet exist. These were excellent motivations for Franz Gruber, the organist, and the priest, Josef Mohr. They got together, with Franz composing the melody and Josef writing the words. Three-and-a-half hours later, the song "Silent Night" was completed. The children's choir sang with Franz and Josef as a guitar accompanied them on Christmas Eve.

The parishioners enjoyed the song immensely. Later, when the organ mender came, he was given a copy of "Silent Night," which he shared from town to town. After 13 years of circulation, "Silent Night" was listed as being written by "author unknown." Next, responsibility for the song was attributed to first one famous composer and then another.

Quite unexpectedly the confusion was straightened out. A choir director at an Austrian school received a letter asking for a copy of "Silent Night." The director, at random, asked one of his students, Felix Gruber, to locate a copy. Felix went home and got one from his father, Franz, who had written the music. After 26 years of obscurity, the real composers finally began to get the proper credit.

It's exciting to come up with a song that everyone enjoys and finds meaningful. But you don't have to be a composer to please God. He finds your personal praise equally as pleasing as the songs of a whole choir. Tell him, "Then will I ever sing praise to your name and fulfill my vows day after day" (Psalm 61:8, NIV). Take some time each day to tell God how much you appreciate his blessings. Even if you can only sing off-key, God will hear the sweetness in your message.

## 156

# Who was Simon in the game Simon Says?

The Simon in the game Simon Says really could say something because he was an actual person. He was a social director at a resort in the early 1900s. He started a fondness in his guests for playing an English game called Wiggle-Waggle, but he changed the name to Do This, Do That. The point of the game was that Simon was in charge. If he told you to do something, you needed to do it exactly, or you were out. If you acted without his permission, you were out also. The guests started calling the game Simon Says.

The object of the game Simon Says is to be the best listener and the one who obeys most exactly. If winning a game seems important while you're playing it, how much more crucial is it to listen to God in life, while you're living it? We are told in the Bible, "You must obey all the commandments of the Lord your God, following his directions in every detail, going the whole way he has laid out for you; only then will you live long and prosperous lives in the land you are to enter and possess" (Deuteronomy 5:32). Use all your listening and understanding skills to play "God Says" each day, and you will always be a winner.

## 157

# How did a dog help save a city?

The city of Nome, Alaska, was desperately waiting for help. In 1925 diphtheria, a fatal disease, was threatening the city. The problem was that the city didn't have enough serum to inoculate its citizens. Extra medicine was 1,000 miles away in Nenana, where the serum had arrived by railroad. Between Nenana and Nome were some small trading posts and an immense amount of barren, snow-covered wilderness. The only way to deliver the medicine would be by dogsled. It would take two weeks, and that would be too long.

A rugged trapper named Wild Bill Shannon strode into the sheriff's office in Nenana with the solution: If each trapping town could have a fresh dog team and driver ready, the serum could be run across the 1,000 miles by relay, cutting the time down to nine days. Within hours, Shannon was on his way with a metal case with 30,000 doses of serum inside. Through the monumental efforts of four relay teams, with their dogs collapsing into the snow at each meeting point, the medicine was passed to the fifth driver, Gunnar Kaasen, on the fifth day. Kaasen was to pass off to one more driver, but because of a blizzard, he missed the trader's cabin where they were to meet. He was on his own.

His lead dog, a Siberian husky named Balto, was well known as an excellent sled dog, and Kaasen was forced by the gigantic snowstorm to rely on Balto's instincts. In the blinding blizzard, at 30 degrees below zero, Kaasen couldn't see the trail. Later, he said, "I gave Balto, my lead dog, his head and trusted him. He never once faltered. The credit is his." Balto pressed on for the next 53 miles. When they reached Nome, Kaasen was almost unconscious, temporarily blinded, and badly cut on his face by ice particles. He had to be chipped from his sled, and the serum was a solid frozen block. It had been delivered in only 144 hours, which saved all but two victims from the diphtheria that could have wiped out an entire city.

You can imagine how tense people were in Nome as they waited for help. There must have been feelings of intense anxiety and yearning and helplessness. Maybe you've been feeling those same feelings. You can't relax, you can't rest, and you can't stop worrying. God doesn't want you to spend your time in that condition. It's not good for you, and it's not necessary.

The Bible says, "For Christ himself is our way of peace" (Ephesians 2:14). If you find yourself wishing that you could be rescued, ask Jesus to be the Lord of your life. Turn your feelings of panic over to him, and ask him to address your problems. He will soothe and comfort and reassure you. He will come to rescue your soul faster and with more power than any human could begin to muster. A blinding snowstorm, a raging fire, or an overwhelming tidal wave couldn't prevent Jesus from rescuing you. Call for him, and he will bring you the medicine for your soul without fail.

## 158

# Why wasn't Miss National Smile Princess smiling?

Miss Moya Ann Church was happy. She had just been voted Miss National Smile Princess for National Smile Week. But it was hard for her to smile that week. First, Moya lost her crown within a minute after being chosen. It was found in a trash pile, but that was only the beginning of her troubles. Someone spilled coffee on her expensive dress and sash, which permanently spoiled them both. Next, she was locked out of her own house by mistake. Then her car broke down. When she went to call for help, her car got a parking ticket. Finally, Moya's week as the National Smile Princess was over. Her picture was taken one last time, and then she missed her train on the way home.

Whenever your happiness depends on the events of your day, it can disappear in a moment. The only way to constantly remain happy is to have your peace of mind dependent on your relationship with Jesus. He says, "As the Father has loved me, so have I loved you. Now remain in my love. If you obey my commands, you will remain in my love, just as I have obeyed my Father's commands and remain in his love. I have told you this so that my joy may be in you and that your joy may be complete" (John 15:9-11, NIV). Add some joy to your day by letting Jesus add some love to your life.

## 159

# How are Social Security numbers selected?

Most of us have memorized our Social Security numbers for one reason or another. Have you ever wondered how they assign these numbers and what yours means? The first three numbers tell which part of the country you lived in when you applied for your card. The smallest numbers, starting with 001, are on the eastern seaboard; the largest numbers are for the Pacific coast. In your Social Security number, the next two numbers stand for the year that you applied for your card. These numbers are in code, so they won't match the year exactly, but the government can read the code. Finally, the last four digits in your Social Security number are your citizen's identification number. Your citizen's number is assigned at random and is kept in government files.

If every single person on earth applied for a Social Security number, eventually we would come to the end of the line, and everyone would have been counted. We would consider that a mammoth project and would be impressed when it was finished. But our human capabilities are so limited; they don't even begin to compare with God's. The Bible says, "He performs wonders that cannot be fathomed, miracles that cannot be counted" (Job 5:9, NIV). Even if every person spent every second counting separate miracles, we still couldn't finish assigning numbers to them. Our God is an infinite God!

---

## 160
# Does sound always travel at the same speed?

There is a definite difference in the speed that sound can travel, depending on what it's traveling through. You would think that since air is thinner than solids, sound would travel faster through air than anything else. Actually, that's not true at all. Air is at the bottom of the list for speedy sound. Air molecules are not tightly packed, so sound waves lose more energy when they travel through air. In one second, sound travels 1,129 feet through air. Through water, it can move about 4,760 feet per second, and through steel or glass it moves 16,000 feet per second. In other words, sound travels fastest through solids, slows down in liquids, and is slowest in gases. The denser the molecules, the faster sound goes through them.

Just as sound can be described in different speeds, the Bible tells us that we should have different speeds in our behavior. It says, "Take note of this: Everyone should be quick to listen, slow to speak and slow to become angry" (James 1:19, NIV). If you concentrate on listening, you will learn a lot. If you think twice before speaking, you might stop yourself from saying something critical or disheartening. And if you keep anger out of your emotions as much as possible, you will be on better terms with everyone you know. Your quality of life will improve immensely if you train yourself when to speed up and when to slow down.

## 161 Does spinach really make you strong?

In the old *Popeye the Sailor* cartoons, Popeye ate a can of spinach and immediately had superhuman strength. Parents told children to eat their spinach so they'd grow up strong like Popeye. It's true that spinach contains iron and that our body needs iron because it builds red blood cells. But spinach does not contain an especially large amount of iron. Our body doesn't even absorb all the iron that is contained in one serving of spinach.

Other foods like enriched breads, lean meats, whole-grain cereals, and liver are just as beneficial in providing iron for our body. In fact, to get all our iron needs from spinach alone, we would have to eat our weight in spinach every day.

Why did spinach get its "strong" reputation? In 1870 a food percentage table was published and widely read. The decimal point for spinach, however, was in the wrong place. The result of this mistake was that spinach seemed to have 10 times more iron than other vegetables. The error stuck in people's minds, and spinach gained its reputation as the vegetable of strength.

It's amazing that people could believe, without question, that a vegetable could make them strong and yet doubt whether God can. God, in fact, is the only way to be truly strong. The Bible says, "Your strength must come from the Lord's mighty power within you" (Ephesians 6:10). The next time you're feeling weak and unable to cope, fuel yourself by opening the Bible instead of a can of spinach.

# 162

## How did stamp collecting start?

Stamp collecting was started by one young woman with an unusual motive. Before the first postal stamps were invented in 1840, people had to take their letters to the post office and pay cash to have them sent. Then the letter was marked "Paid" and sent on its way.

The first stamp was sold in England and was called a "Penny Black." It was decorated with a picture of the head of Queen Victoria. In 1841 the young lady of our story had an idea. She placed an advertisement in the *London Times*, asking people to send her their used stamps. Why would anybody want those? She merely wanted to use them to change her room—the stamps would be her new wallpaper!

The idea of reusing stamps as wallpaper may qualify as one of the first recycling projects. Even Jesus was concerned about being careful with leftovers. Jesus fed the crowds with loaves and fishes that kept multiplying until everyone was full. "'Now gather the scraps,' Jesus told his disciples, 'so that nothing is wasted'" (John 6:12). When we treat our blessings with respect, it shows God that we are appreciative of his abundant gifts.

# What secrets are some statues saying?

When you see a statue of a man sitting on a horse, you probably don't realize that the sculptor is giving you a clue about how the man died. Although this doesn't apply to every statue, it has long been a tradition to position the horse by a type of code. If the horse has all four feet on the ground, its rider died from natural causes. If one of the horse's hooves is raised, it indicates that the rider eventually died from wounds he received in a battle. If the horse is rearing up with both front hooves in the air, the rider died right on the battlefield.

Death is an important milestone in human history. We pay attention to how it happens to others. Maybe that's because we know that one day it will happen to us, and we want to learn as much as we can. All we really need to know is that we will not be alone. God has promised that he will *never* leave us. We can say with confidence, "Even when walking through the dark valley of death I will not be afraid, for you are close beside me, guarding, guiding all the way" (Psalm 23:4). Even if no one ever erects a statue of you, if you're God's child, everyone will already know how you died—securely cast in his love.

## 164

# Why does the man walk next to the curb when escorting a woman?

The street can be a hazardous place. Vehicles can splash puddle water onto your clothes or veer threateningly close to the curb. City street gutters can be full of unpleasant debris. The custom of men walking next to the street came about because people in the early days threw trash and emptied chamber pots out of the windows above. Pedestrians walking below were likely to get a dirty shower. A gentleman was expected to take the side of the sidewalk closest to the street, in order to protect the lady he was accompanying from every danger.

It's a good idea to have someone keep their eye on every step we take so that our feet won't come down in the wrong place. Living within God's love is like that. Your steps will be carefully watched, so you can avoid the dangers. But it's God who will be doing the guarding. You can turn over your anxieties to him. The Bible says, "He sees everything I do and every step I take" (Job 31:4). It can be a wonderful feeling to know that someone loves you so much that he's got you on his arm, watches where you go, and paves the way ahead of you.

# Can you name one number that never changes?

You'll need a pencil and paper for this exercise, but you'll probably find it intriguing enough to make the effort. This is the story of the "sum that's always the same." No matter how many times you try these few steps, you will always arrive at the same answer. Here's how it works:

1. Pick any three-digit number, making sure that the first digit is larger than the last (975, for example).
2. Reverse the number you picked (579).
3. Subtract the smaller number (579) from the larger number (975). If your calculations leave you with a two-digit number, like 99, add a zero to the beginning of the number (099).
4. Take the answer from step 3 (975-579=396) and reverse it (693).
5. Add together the answer for step 3 (396) and its reverse (693).
6. You will *always* end up with the number 1089.

We like counting, perhaps, because it makes us feel that we have some control over things and that we can define them. But no one can define, count, or limit the goodness of God. His children say, "O Lord my God, many and many a time you have done great miracles for us, and we are ever in your thoughts. Who else can do such glorious things? No one else can be compared with you" (Psalm 40:5).

## 166

# Why would anyone ask the enemy for advice during a war?

An extraordinary thing happened during the Civil War. Colonel John T. Wilder was leading a battalion that had the first repeating rifles, which were bought by the men themselves. But even the new weapons couldn't help them in 1862. The colonel knew that his men were surrounded and outnumbered. He thought about surrendering, but he wasn't sure if that was the right thing to do. There was no one he could ask, except for the commander of the enemy forces.

So that is what Colonel Wilder did. He waved a white flag and walked across the battlefield to the camp as the Confederates watched. He was escorted to General Bragg. Colonel Wilder asked the general what would be the best thing for his troops to do. The general told the colonel that it would be a good idea to count how many cannons were pointed at his men that very moment. Colonel Wilder counted to 46, stopped counting, and surrendered. More than 4,000 men's lives were saved that day.

As with many things, surrendering is viewed differently on earth than it is in heaven. People usually equate a surrender with a failure. But when you surrender your will to God, you can consider it a victory. The Bible says, "Give yourselves completely to God—every part of you—for you are back from death and you want to be tools in the hands of God, to be used for his good purposes" (Romans 6:13). When you ask God to fill your soul, you surrender yourself and become better than you were. And you've saved a life—your own.

## 167
# What's the story behind the Taj Mahal?

If you've ever heard someone say, "You act like you live in the Taj Mahal," maybe you've wondered what they mean. It all began in the 1600s. The emperor Shah Jahan of India built the monument as a tomb for the wife he loved and lost. She died after 20 years of a happy marriage while giving birth to their 14th child. Her name was Mumtaz Mahal, and "Taj Mahal" is a shortened version of her name. It means "Chosen One of the Palace."

The palace was built on the banks of the Jumna River by 22,000 men over the course of 22 years. The emperor planned to build his own tomb out of black marble across the river, to be connected to the Taj Mahal by a silver bridge. But that never happened because Shah Jahan was imprisoned by his own son during a political coup. When the emperor died, he was laid to rest in the Taj Mahal next to his wife.

The Taj Mahal is an octagon that includes six domes, elaborate gardens, a long pool, a tall sandstone gate, and many decorations made from gemstones. Just one flower on one wall could have as many as 60 pieces of inlaid gems. For its time, the Taj Mahal was recognized as one of the most elaborate structures in the world.

The Taj Mahal was the way that the emperor chose to remind people of his wife. Her memory will endure as long as the building does—which won't be forever. But God does not need a building or a memorial or anything visible to remind people about him. The Bible says, "O Jehovah, your name endures forever; your fame is known to every generation" (Psalm 135:13). God's legacy is passed from parent to child to grandchild because God's promises are the most precious gifts we can share with those we love.

# 168
# How was masking tape invented?

If people hadn't wanted to buy fancy cars, masking tape might never have been invented. In 1902 a new company was started called the Minnesota Mining and Manufacturing Company—3M for short. 3M wanted to dig for a mineral called corundum and sell it to companies that made sandpaper. But 3M made two mistakes.

While they were trying to mine the mineral, a better way to make sandpaper was invented. Suddenly no one needed corundum anymore. Not only that, but 3M found out that the mine they had built didn't even have any corundum in it. 3M almost went out of business right then, but it decided instead to try to make its own sandpaper.

To make sure that their sandpaper was the best, 3M's salesmen went into the factories and asked the workers what they needed most. Since 3M's biggest customers for sandpaper would be people who worked on auto bodies, 3M found out about a big problem that the car builders had. The newest cars were supposed to have two different colors painted on them, but the painters couldn't get clear, straight lines between the two colors. They had tried covering one color up with newspaper while they sprayed the other color on. But the newspaper had to be glued to the car and wouldn't come off the side of the car without pulling the paint off, too. 3M solved the problem by inventing a tan-colored tape that wouldn't take off the paint but did make a sharp line between colors.

The man most responsible for this project was Richard G. Drew. But 3M made yet another mistake. To save money, 3M didn't put enough stickiness on the back of the tape, so it tended to fall off the car. The painters said that 3M was like the Scotch people, who were said to be good at saving money. 3M put more stickiness onto their tape, and the workers started using what they had nick-named "Scotch" tape. 3M kept that name for all of its products.

When we need to mend something, the name *Scotch* comes to mind. When we need hope, the name *Jesus* is recognized. The Bible says, "Salvation is found in no one else, for there is no other name under heaven given to men by which we must be saved" (Acts 4:12, NIV).

# 169
# What was brewing over the tea bag?

The next time you're boiling water and brewing your tea bags, think of Thomas Sullivan.

Sullivan was a tea salesman in the early 1900s. He sent samples of his tea to customers, either in tins or in paper packets. The loose tea leaves, once unwrapped, fell out all over, and customers never really got to try the tea. Sullivan decided to send his samples in hand-sewn miniature silk bags instead. All the customer had to do was drop the bag in boiling water and enjoy. After Sullivan sent the bags, he got many orders for his tea—but the customers only wanted the tea if it came in the little bags. They loved the convenience, and Thomas Sullivan became the surprised inventor of the tea bag.

Jesus had an example about containers, meant to make us think about how our life is changed once we have invited him in. Jesus said, "You know better than to put new wine into old wineskins. They would burst. The wine would be spilled out and the wineskins ruined. New wine needs fresh wineskins" (Mark 2:22). Jesus meant that his presence changes everything. We can't expect to keep the old rules or remain our old selves once his love comes to us. We are transformed, as thoroughly as the tea business was transformed by the appearance of the tea bag. There's no going back to the old way.

——————————— **170**

# How does thunder get stolen?

When you want to be the one to announce some big news, but someone else beats you to it, you can say that he "stole your thunder." This phrase does refer to the "noise" created by thunder, but there's a little more to the story.

It was John Dennis who coined the phrase in 1709, and he meant it literally. He was an English playwright who invented a new way of simulating the sound of thunder on the stage by using wooden troughs. The play he created the sound effects for didn't last, but the idea of his thunder did. Dennis went to see another play and recognized the sounds of his creation. He exclaimed, "The villains will not play my play, but they steal my thunder!" Since then the phrase has come to express disappointment at anything that keeps you from getting the attention you feel rightly belongs to you.

No one will ever be able to steal God's thunder. The Bible asks, "Do you have an arm like God's, and can your voice thunder like his?" (Job 40:9, NIV). The attention of man will always be on God because no one can imitate his power. He created the thunder that we can only weakly copy. God is "larger than life."

## 171

# Why do men wear neckties?

Neckties today really don't serve a purpose, except to allow men to express a little of their personalities through color or style. Neckties, which were really more like scarves, first were worn by the soldiers of ancient Rome for a specific reason. Those ties made good neck warmers in cold weather and good perspiration absorbers in heated climates. There was also a fluffy collar called a "ruff" before 1660. That's the year when men's neckwear changed.

The new style came from Croatian soldiers who came to Paris and marched in a parade. Each soldier had a bright handkerchief around his neck, which the French began to copy. This was eventually called a *cravat*—French for "Croatian." Some cravats were worn with wire in them to make them stiff or were filled with cushions to make them puffy. Many were worn so tightly around the neck that a man couldn't even turn his head. When the French were fighting in the French Revolution, ties changed again.

The English attacked by surprise. The French at that time were wearing their handkerchiefs in a "slide," like the Boy Scouts' scarf. The French soldiers didn't have time to slide the cloth through, so they quickly knotted their handkerchiefs around their necks, inadvertently starting a new fad. The French won the battle, and neckties became popular for all men, who wore their neckties to show by the color which side of the Revolution they supported. After that, wearing ties became a custom. The fashionable knotted tie started in 1920, when it was designed by joining four pieces of cloth cut on a slant so that they wouldn't get twisted.

A tie is an outward sign that a man is respecting the "rules" of appropriate dress. God asks us to give outward signs of our respect for his commandments by obeying them. The Bible says, "Obeying these commandments is not something beyond your strength and reach; for these laws are not in the far heavens, so distant that you can't hear and obey them, and with no one to bring them down to you; nor are they beyond the ocean, so far that no one can bring you their message; but they are very close at hand—in your hearts and on your lips—so obey them" (Deuteronomy 30:11-14). In other words, the rules for godly living are as available to you as the rules about how to dress every day. When you put on your tie on the outside, remember to put God's words on the inside.

# 172
## Why were wedding rings collected at a tollbooth?

You have traffic waiting impatiently in line behind you, the Golden Gate Bridge in San Francisco spans before you, and the tollbooth requires some money that you don't have. Now what? Fortunately for many commuters, you are allowed to leave something else in place of money, as long as it is equal to or exceeds the toll. That is how the tollbooth acquired such a strange collection of objects.

In exchange for being allowed to cross the bridge, drivers have left a can of motor oil, a frying pan, a set of silverware, a new book, and rock and roll music. Wedding rings are often left, mostly by men. An older gentleman left his dentures, but he came back to claim them the next day. A diamond wristwatch worth $7,000 still hadn't been picked up years later and was sold at an auction for $5. The only things that the tollbooth won't take are animals, uncanned food, or clothes. One man offered to leave his dog, but only the collar was kept by the tollbooth attendant. There was a young man who offered to pay with marijuana. He didn't get to make the trip across the bridge. Instead, he went to jail.

We understand how the tollbooth works: We give something of value in exchange for the privilege of going to another place. That's exactly what Jesus did for us: He paid the price so that we could have the privilege of going to heaven. The Bible says, "You know that it was not with perishable things such as silver or gold that you were redeemed from the empty way of life handed down to you from your forefathers, but with the precious blood of Christ, a lamb without blemish or defect" (1 Peter 1:18-19, NIV). You are so important to Christ that he said, "You can go forward at no cost, and I'll pay the highest price." No one else could love you so much.

## 173
# Why was a tomato taken to trial?

In 1893 the Supreme Court put a tomato on trial. The case came about because of a law that said fruits could be brought into America without a tax, but importers had to pay for vegetables. John Nix was taxed for the load of tomatoes he brought to New York, and he took his tomatoes to court. Scientists and botanists, he said, would testify that the tomato was really a fruit. The Court explored the legal definition of a tomato and arrived at a strange decision.

The judges said that by nature, tomatoes were fruits of the vine. Just like berries (as well as squash, beans, peas, and cucumbers, which are often thought of as vegetables), tomatoes have seeds inside a pulpy, juicy tissue. Even though the tomato is botanically classified as a fruit, the way people ate it made it officially a vegetable. They served the tomato with dinner, rather than as a dessert. The tax was valid under the tomato law.

This case was based on semantics, or what the words *vegetable* and *fruit* really mean. No matter what its official definition is, we're still going to recognize it as a tomato or a grape or a squash when we pick it. The Bible uses examples about vegetation to teach us how to distinguish God's people from those who aren't Christians.

It says, "You can detect them by the way they act, just as you can identify a tree by its fruit. You need never confuse grapevines with thorn bushes or figs with thistles. Different kinds of fruit trees can quickly be identified by examining their fruit. A variety that produces delicious fruit never produces an inedible kind. And a tree producing an inedible kind can't produce what is good. So the trees having the inedible fruit are chopped down and thrown on the fire. Yes, the way to identify a tree or a person is by the kind of fruit produced" (Matthew 7:16-20). The lesson is: Don't judge people's sincerity by what they say. Look at how they live their lives. And expect that people will be watching you in the same way. God's children should be living in such a way that their lives are constructive, beneficial, honest, and wholesome.

## 174

# Why does the Leaning Tower of Pisa lean?

The Leaning Tower of Pisa is a famous Italian landmark. It was built as part of a church just before the Renaissance, which was a period of great cultural growth. The tower is round and measures 179 feet high. It leans about 16 feet to one side, and it is leaning more each year.

The problem started because the tower was built on ground that was not solid. Even as it was being built, it was starting to sink. The builder tried making the next stories taller on one side, but the tower leaned even more because of the extra weight. Building stopped completely for 100 years while everyone studied the problem. Finally two more stories were built out of line with the rest of the building, but still the tower leaned. Its marble columns are beginning to disintegrate, but the Leaning Tower of Pisa is expected to remain standing for centuries.

Many people have tried to think of ways to straighten the tower. Among the letters sent to Pisa each week, there has even been a suggestion to tie balloons to the top of the tower to lift it up. Once, holes were dug underneath the lowest side of the tower, and the holes were filled with 900 tons of cement. But the building just tilted more. The city has chosen to leave the famous tower leaning because of the attention it continues to create.

The Leaning Tower of Pisa is special because it is so unusual—it should have fallen over by now, as most crooked buildings would. Someday it will topple because the ground underneath has never been sturdy.

Jesus used an example that we can understand. He said, "All who listen to my instructions and follow them are wise, like a man who builds his house on solid rock. Though the rain comes in torrents, and the floods rise and the storm winds beat against his house, it won't collapse, for it is built on rock. But those who hear my instructions and ignore them are foolish, like a man who builds his house on sand. For when the rains and floods come, and storm winds beat against his house, it will fall with a mighty crash" (Matthew 7:24-27). Don't count on being able to lean like the tower of Pisa. Make sure you've got your foundation straight with God.

## 175

# Why do police cars use blue lights?

There are some facts about cars that you may not know. One concerns your own car, along with everyone else's. Why do all the doors swing open toward the front of the car instead of the back? The answer is "aerodynamics."

When you drive, air pressure builds up around your moving car. If the doors swung toward the back, there would be a higher chance that the air pressure could force your door to open unexpectedly. When door latches weren't as sturdy as they are now, that was a real concern. Because the air streams around your car from front to back, having the doors open toward the rear allows the use of air pressure to help keep them closed.

Now consider the police car. Why are police cars the only emergency vehicles to have blue lights mixed in with, or replacing, the red? At one time, emergency vehicles all had red lights only. The police encountered a problem when they were signaling a car to stop. Sometimes the car would continue moving, and the driver would claim that he was "just trying to get out of the way." The driver then established an alibi, and the most he could be charged with was "failing to yield to an emergency vehicle." Because police vehicles have added blue flashing lights, there can be no mistaking who's behind you. Incidentally, blue was picked instead of another color because it is easily seen.

Laws are often motivated by a concern for your welfare. The laws about rear-swinging car doors are to protect you from falling out. You're to stop for the police because they're trying to keep you from endangering others by breaking laws. Without laws, there would be chaos. Maybe you have experienced that kind of chaos in your own life. There is no order, plan, or purpose. That's because you aren't close enough to God to be under the protection of his laws.

The Bible says, "God's laws are perfect. They protect us, make us wise, and give us joy and light. God's laws are pure, eternal, just. They are more desirable than gold. They are sweeter than honey dripping from a honeycomb. For they warn us away from harm and give success to those who obey them" (Psalm 19:7-11). Search the Bible to learn the rules that will point you toward peace, calmness, and security.

# What historical stories do nursery rhymes tell?

Most nursery rhymes came about for a reason—they were actually a way of telling stories. Time has erased the history behind these tales, so the words of nursery rhymes often seem like childish gibberish to us. We teach them to our children as innocent, fun games of childhood. Because the words didn't seem to make much sense, you may have learned a slightly different version of the poem "Ring-a-ring o' roses, / A pocket full of posies. / Aitchoo! Aitchoo! / We all fall down." The true meaning may surprise you.

This poem is actually a gruesome description of the process of becoming a victim of the Black Plague. This disease swept Europe in the fourteenth century and in 1665 had a resurgence in England, where this rhyme originated. The symptoms started with red spots and rashes (Ring-a-ring o' roses). People believed that this plague was caused by the breath of evil demons, and they thought that flowers would sweeten the air and keep sickness away (A pocket full of posies). The next symptom of illness was sneezing (Aitchoo!), and finally death came (We all fall down).

And what about that other familiar favorite, "Jack and Jill"? It's believed that this poem is describing the motions of the ocean tide. When the tide comes up to the shore, Jack and Jill go up the hill—both pulled by the moon. As the tide surges back out to the ocean with the weakening of the moon's pull, Jack and Jill can't stay up on the hill and tumble also.

Almost all parents teach nursery rhymes to their children. We also make sure that they practice their alphabet, their manners, their spelling, tying their shoelaces, and their piano lessons. That's because we want them to become prepared for life. We want to help them get ahead. But if you are involved in the raising of children, don't neglect what will help them the most. Make sure that they know Jesus. He says, "Let the little children come to me, and do not hinder them, for the kingdom of God belongs to such as these" (Mark 10:14, NIV).

Before the karate class, the soccer team, or the computer club, enroll them in Sunday school, take them to church, and talk to them about God. Having God in their lives will enhance their talents and give them the peace and reassurance of a firm foundation. That, in turn, will free them to pursue excellence in other areas.

## 177
# Why did the president's son take a book to the inauguration?

Most of us are familiar with the children's book *Treasure Island*, written by Robert Lewis Stevenson. He described his book as a story "all about a map, and a treasure, and a mutiny, and a derelict ship . . . and a sea-cook with one leg. . . ." How does an author come up with such an imaginative work? Stevenson even surprised himself with the idea.

He was entertaining his stepson one rainy day by drawing a treasure map. When the child begged for explanations to match the pictures, Stevenson made up some stories. He liked what he told his stepson and made copies of the tales he told. With a few changes, these ideas became the novel *Treasure Island*. Perhaps the highest praise for Stevenson's book came from a president's son. When President Taft was making his inauguration speech, his son Charlie—obligated to attend the inauguration but convinced he would be bored—chose to bring along the book he thought would be more interesting than his father's acceptance of the presidency: a copy of *Treasure Island*.

If Charlie liked stories about looking for real treasure, he was reading the wrong book. The most valuable thing we can "find" on earth is not gold but the rewards of God's love. The place to look for those is in the Bible, which says, "The Kingdom of Heaven is like a treasure a man discovered in a field. In his excitement, he sold everything he owned to get enough money to buy the field—and get the treasure, too!" (Matthew 13:44). Now that's a treasure hunt worth pursuing!

# Who wouldn't accept a check from the treasury secretary?

It pays to be secretary of the United States Department of the Treasury, as Michael Blumenthal found out in 1979. Secretary Blumenthal was in an embarrassing predicament. He had just enjoyed an elaborate and expensive meal at a restaurant in San Francisco. He gave the waiter his credit card, and the waiter returned with the news that the card had expired and couldn't be used for payment. The secretary next offered to pay by check.

Unfortunately, the establishment needed a guarantee on the signature before it could accept an out-of-town check. Instead of being worried, this is when Blumenthal could relax. Verifying his signature was easy. He pulled a dollar bill out of his wallet and showed the waiter the signature in the corner of the bill. There it was—W. M. Blumenthal. Just to be sure, the waiter compared the signatures. They were, of course, a perfect match, and the secretary's check was accepted with no further questions.

When someone recognizes your name and knows who you are, it gives you a powerful feeling. If you think earthly recognition is a thrill, anticipate how glorious it will be when you are acknowledged in heaven. The Bible says, "Rejoice that your names are written in heaven" (Luke

10:20, NIV). It is much more important to gain access to eternity than it is to gain entrance into a restaurant. Live your life so that when your time comes, God will say, "Yes, I recognize the name of this one. This one belongs here with me and is entitled to all the privileges of heaven."

# 179

# How did the washing machine change wash day?

If it seems like you're always doing laundry, you probably are. One thing's for sure—you're doing it a lot more often than your ancestors did. In the seventeenth century, clothes were washed about four or five times a year. One hundred years later, the average wash day came around every five or six weeks. Some clothes were never washed because they were made of satin, brocade, silk, and velvet. The washable clothes were hard enough to get clean. If you were a sailor, you could just drop your clothes over the side of the boat in a net and haul them back up when they'd been in the water long enough. But for most people, there was a lot more effort involved in washing.

Rubbing clothes on rocks or sand in the river and laying them out to dry on bushes was one way to do laundry. When washing moved inside, water had to be hauled in from out-

side, then heated over a fire and poured into additional tubs.
Rinsing required even more water. There was the scrub board
and then the squeezing and wringing out of every piece of
clothing. In the early 1800s the wringer, which was turned by
a handle, appeared. In 1859 Hamilton E. Smith came up with
a better idea. He patented a washtub that had paddles that
were turned by a hand crank. Then in 1874 Bill Blackstone
put six pegs in the bottom of a washtub, connected them to a
rotating handle-and-gear mechanism, and invented what's
been called the first washing machine. Blackstone had created
an uncommon appliance, but what he did with it was all too
common. He presented it to his wife on her birthday. By
1922 America was making electric washing machines, which
housewives in foreign countries used with great creativity.
During World War II, Dutch women used the washers as substitute butter churns, and island women used them to tender-
ize their octopus dinners.

Because wash days used to be so taxing, it must have been
a monumental relief when you knew everything was finally
clean and fresh, and you were ready to begin again. Maybe
you feel your life is very draining, too. You would welcome
the feeling that all the bad things in your past had been
washed away and you had been given the chance to start all
over. Jesus offers you that opportunity, any time you're
ready to take it. The Bible says, "When someone becomes a
Christian, he becomes a brand new person inside. He is not
the same any more. A new life has begun!" (2 Corinthians
5:17). If you haven't asked Jesus to be the Lord of your life,
you're living with a lot of dirty laundry. Just by telling him,
"Jesus, I want you to take over now," your whole life can be

clean again. Why not make today the most important "wash day" of your life?

## 180

# Who wanted the same birthday present every year?

Everybody likes birthday presents, but possibly the most unique gift ever received was one that an Englishman, Isambard Kingdom Brunel, gave himself. Brunel was a design engineer in the 1800s. He worked on the plans for a railroad tunnel to be built in England. He figured out that he could change the specifications slightly and give himself a personal treat. On only one day a year, when the sun rose in the morning, it brilliantly lit up the inside of the tunnel. Which day was it? April 9—Brunel's birthday.

Brunel waited eagerly for dawn on his birthday to receive his special gift. We, too, can receive a special gift of light, and we should search every bit as eagerly for it. The Bible says, "When you consider the wonderful truth of the prophets' words, then the light will dawn in your souls and Christ the Morning Star will shine in your hearts" (2 Peter 1:19). Imagine the most glorious dawn, and see yourself filled with it. That's how you look to God when you believe in his Son.

# Does your kitchen contain this invention?

Earl Tupper—does his name sound familiar? You probably have something of his in your kitchen because Earl Tupper created Tupperware.

Tupper started out his sales career as a boy, selling vegetables that other kids had grown because he could make more money than growing the vegetables himself. As an adult, Tupper worked for DuPont and had a mail-order business on the side, selling toothbrushes and combs. When his business allowed him to retire from DuPont, he began experimenting with polyethylene. He succeeded in 1945 with an invention he called Poly T. It was a big improvement over the plastic of the late 1930s, which cracked because it was so rigid. To avoid high advertising costs, Tupperware "parties" became the best way to sell his new product. Women hosted their neighbors at home demonstrations. The first piece of Tupperware was a seven-ounce bathroom tumbler. Then came the bowls with airtight lids. Everybody wanted some, from institutions to corporations to museums. Tupper became wealthy and sold out to Rexall Drugs in 1958.

If you have something tucked away in a Tupperware container, you've already decided it's worth the effort to make sure you can save it. God has only one thing he wants saved. The Bible tells us, "The Lord preserves the faithful" (Psalm 31:23, NIV). A Tupperware container can save something for a while, but God's saving of your soul will endure throughout eternity. Let God become your Keeper!

## 182

# Who was "Typhoid Mary"?

Mary Mallon made people sick—literally. In 1897 Mary went to work as a cook for a family in New York. Everyone was impressed with her talents, but it only took 10 days for them to change their minds. The whole household contracted typhoid fever, and it came from Mary. She didn't have typhoid herself, but she spread it to others because she was a carrier.

She was also a fugitive. She disappeared from the New York house in the middle of the night and stayed one step ahead of the law for the next 10 years. Using aliases, she worked her way through Massachusetts, New York, and Maine, always leaving sickness in her wake. She earned the nickname "Typhoid Mary." Finally, she was located, but the official who went to talk to her escaped with his life after being attacked with a carving fork. It took five police officers to subdue her and place her in a mental hospital.

She was let out after promising that she would stay away from food service. However, people started getting sick again, and her trail led to a hospital, where she was discovered working in the maternity ward. This time she was institutionalized until her death. No one knows whether she didn't understand how dangerous she was or just didn't care. Either way, many people became sick because she infected them.

Typhoid Mary did not act responsibly nor according to God's will, and you can see the trouble it caused. Jesus said, "Love your neighbor as much as you love yourself" (Matthew 22:39). Mary undoubtedly would not have wanted someone else to make her sick, so she shouldn't have been spreading sickness to others. When you love someone else as much as yourself, you will wish only good for them. You will strive to nurture, protect, and encourage them. Imagine what a wonderful world we would have if everyone in it sincerely "put the other guy" first!

# 183
# Why are veins blue when blood is red?

Blood in your body makes an amazing round-trip. It starts in your lungs, where it gets lots of oxygen. The oxygen gets mixed within the red blood cells with hemoglobin, which is also red. Now the blood, which is bright red because its color has been intensified by oxygen and hemoglobin, travels through the arteries. Arteries are thick, strong tubes that help the blood reach the rest of your body, where it delivers the oxygen it's carrying. Along the way, blood deposits oxygen to your tissues.

When all the oxygen has been distributed to the different parts of your body, your blood is ready to make the return trip back to your lungs to fill itself back up with more oxygen. The way blood travels to your heart and then back through your lungs is through the veins. Veins are thinner and more transparent than arteries, which is why you can see your blood through them. The blood appears blue or purplish because it no longer has oxygen in it. The color of blood "fades" until more oxygen is added.

Jesus had ordinary blood like ours, yet his was one-of-a-kind. His blood is the most potent that ever flowed. The Bible says, "If we are living in the light of God's presence, just as Christ does, then we have wonderful fellowship and joy with each other, and the blood of Jesus his Son cleanses us from every sin" (1 John 1:7). We always think of blood as staining; yet the blood of Jesus is the only thing that can clean the stains in our souls.

# 184
# Why is the bottom button of a man's vest left undone?

Men don't button the bottom button of a vest or a suit coat. It's a custom, taught from fathers to sons. But where did it come from? All the buttons on vests and coats were buttoned until the late 1700s. It was the Prince of Wales, who was in line to become king, who started this fashion statement. He always left the bottom buttons undone, and men copied his ways, hoping to appear more kingly themselves. The Prince of Wales wasn't trying to change the fashion industry. He was just trying to be comfortable. His large stomach wouldn't quite fit into the buttoned clothes. Because the prince was overweight, men of all sizes and shapes have been unbuttoning ever since.

When buttoning their vests, men probably don't stop to ask why they're doing it. But there are many times in our life when we do want to ask God what he's doing. Why did I lose my loved one? Why did I lose my job? Why did I make such a big mistake? Often we feel that there can't have been a good reason for something that hurt us so much. But our mind is limited to human thoughts. Only God can see the whole picture. The Bible says, "There is a time for everything, and a season for every activity under heaven" (Ecclesiastes 3:1, NIV). You can have peace when you accept that God is in charge, that he has knowledge and wisdom far beyond our own, and that he is worthy of our trust.

## 185

# When did a solution become a growing problem?

Soil was a problem in the southern United States. It was constantly eroding, or washing away. After many frustrating years, a solution appeared. It was the kudzu vine, native to Asia. This vine had deep roots that held the soil in place. It grew quickly, and it even put nitrogen back into the soil. Farmers received cuttings of the vine free from the Soil Conservation Service. Entire communities got together to plant the kudzu vine throughout their cities and towns. Everyone was excited about how the vine would save the soil.

But that's not what happened. Instead, the plant made things much worse. The vine grew so fast, it could cover a foot a day in every direction. It grew four feet down into the ground. It clung to gardens, buildings, utility poles—anything and everything in its path. The kudzu vine was out of control. Chain saws, chemicals, hatchets, or even fire couldn't stop it. Every spring it begins to grow again. Kudzu can be found across seven million acres in the South.

Farmers don't want the kudzu to be fruitful or to multiply any more. But there is a good vine that everyone should hope will prosper all over the world. Jesus says," I am the true Vine, and my Father is the Gardener. He lops off every branch that doesn't produce. And he prunes those branches that bear fruit for even larger crops. He has already tended you by pruning you back for greater strength and usefulness by means of the commands I gave you. Take care to live in me, and let me live in you. For a branch can't produce fruit when severed from the vine. Nor can you be fruitful apart from me. Yes, I am the Vine; you are the branches. Whoever lives in me and I in him shall produce a large crop of fruit" (John 15:1-5). When Jesus covers the earth like a vine, it won't be considered a problem. Instead, it will be an occasion for rejoicing—and you can help it happen.

# 186

# How do you interpret the results of a vision test?

Most of us have had our eyes tested enough to know that 20/20 means perfect vision and that numbers higher than this mean our vision is less than perfect. Only one out of every three people has 20/20 vision. But do you know what the numbers stand for? The first number will always be 20, and it means a distance of 20 feet. That's how far away the chart is that you're tested on. If your eye tests 20/20, it means that you are reading normal letters at 20 feet that a person with perfect vision can also see at 20 feet.

The second number is the one that compares your vision to everyone else's. When your eye tests at 20/40, that means that you can only see letters at 20 feet away that other people with perfect vision can see from 40 feet away. Each of your eyes will have its own set of numbers. As you get older, your ability to see things clearly in the distance will remain better longer than your ability to see things close-up.

No matter how poor your eyesight may be, you won't ever need to worry about missing the most important thing in life. It's guaranteed in the Bible, which says, "Unto them that look for him shall he appear" (Hebrews 9:28, KJV). Jesus will always be near enough to you that you can find him. Focus your attention on his Word, and he will help you to see all the benefits that will be yours when you become his child.

# 187

# What was the best investment that was ever made on Wall Street?

History tells us that buying the land on which Wall Street sits (on the island of Manhattan in New York City) was probably the best deal ever made there. The governor of the Dutch settlement that wanted to settle on the island bought the land for twenty-four dollars' worth of cloth, trinkets, and beads, which he traded to the Indians.

We hear the name "Wall Street" almost daily because it is the financial capital of America. It's natural to assume that the skyscrapers lining the street formed a brick and concrete wall to give the street its name. But the name "Wall Street" has been around since 1653—long before there were any multistory buildings. Where did the name come from?

At one time there really was an old earthen wall right down the middle of what became Wall Street. It was built there by the Dutch after they traded for the land. They settled on the lower section of Manhattan Island, forming the oldest borough of New York City. Worried about being invaded, specifically by the Indians or the English, the Dutch built the wall to protect their real estate investment. By the way, the first location of the New York Stock Exchange on Wall Street was in the Tontine Coffee House, and once in a while the brokers met under a tree.

Sometimes people build emotional walls, which can be hurtful. Maybe you've had a disagreement with someone, and you're no longer speaking. Maybe you've been hurt, and you're going to keep everyone away, even though they love you. God can help you mend the rifts in your life. The Bible says, "For he himself is our peace, who has made the two one and has destroyed the barrier, the dividing wall of hostility" (Ephesians 2:14, NIV). Start your quest for God's peace. He will help you take the walls down brick by brick.

## 188

# Why would a family throw glass balls at a fire?

We really don't know how man learned to use fire. Lightning probably started a fire in a forest, and man may have picked up a burning piece of wood and started a fire in the spot of his choosing. We do know that after man realized fires were good for keeping warm and chasing animals away, he made sure to keep his fire going. He didn't know yet how to start a new one. Throughout history we have learned much more about fire. For instance, not all fires cause smoke. If you see smoke, it means that unburned materials are floating into the air. If everything in the flames is being totally consumed, there will be no smoke. We also know that the hardest fires to put out are those that are burning cork or rubber. Learning how to stop a fire was a long process.

In 1734 a German doctor put saline solution into glass balls. He suggested that those who found their house on fire should throw these balls into the flames, where they would burst and start extinguishing it. Then in 1816 a Scottish man invented a copper canister filled with compressed air, potassium carbonate, and water after witnessing a fire where no one above the fifth floor could be helped. This canister allowed people to start controlling a fire themselves until additional help could arrive.

Getting a fire under control has remained a big problem.

Sometimes it can't be stopped, even though all known extinguishers are used. The Bible compares our tongues with a fire out of control. It says, "The tongue is a small thing, but what enormous damage it can do. A great forest can be set on fire by one tiny spark" (James 3:5). Once something is said, it is almost impossible to take it back. If you are lying or gossiping, you may become the source of destruction of your own reputation or someone else's. Think carefully about what you say because even the smallest word—the tiniest spark—can be fanned by others into a raging fire that no one can control.

## 189

# Why was someone ironing dollar bills?

During the years of 1912 to 1916, if someone handed you a crisp one-dollar bill, it had probably just been freshly ironed. Yes, ironed, as in what happens to clothes after they've been washed. Who would iron money? The United States Department of the Treasury.

During that time, bills were in short supply. A study showed that most used bills were simply dirty, rather than unusable. To save expenses, the Treasury Department decided to wash the old money. A machine was built that could wash 40,000 bills a day and that two people could operate. Two long conveyor belts moved the money into some germicide and soapy water. Then the bills were dried. Finally, the money was ironed and put back into circulation.

The next time currency became a problem was during World War I. Until that time bills had been made out of linen, which suddenly became rare. The Treasury Department made the paper money out of cotton instead, but that faded too much to be washed. After the war, it was suggested that linen money and the washing process be started again. That's when the Secret Service stepped in and announced that "washed" money was easier to mix up with counterfeit. The Treasury Department burned bills until the 1970s and then switched to a shredder to remove more than $51 billion from circulation in the next three years alone.

The Treasury Department tries its hardest to keep people from counterfeiting. But there will always be deceitful people working even harder to beat the system. Maybe you've run across someone who has tried to cheat you. God will deal with him. The Bible says, "He frustrates the plans of crafty men. They are caught in their own traps; he thwarts their schemes" (Job 5:12-13). Don't seek revenge because that would result in your becoming crafty yourself. God knows the best way to deal with and conquer evil.

## 190

# Who tried to control the ocean?

In England in the eleventh century, King Canute wanted to prove a point. He went down to the ocean shore and stood on the beach, commanding the waves not to rise. King Canute wasn't suffering from an inflated ego. Quite the opposite was true. He wanted his subjects to see that God has powers much greater than any man.

As the king stood on the shore, the waves advanced until the incoming tide was swirling around is feet. That's when he announced to his people that no one on earth was worthy to be called "king." The only king, he said, was God, "whose nod heaven and earth and sea obey under laws eternal." To emphasize the lesson, King Canute took off his crown and never wore it again. Instead, he hung it on a crucifix above the head of Jesus.

By being humble, King Canute was being a better ruler. He was directing his subjects toward God, urging them to acknowledge what the Bible teaches: "You rule the oceans when their waves arise in fearful storms; you speak, and they lie still" (Psalm 89:9). Just as he should, the king was bowing to the King of kings.

# 191

## Where goes
## the bride?

Technically, most brides have no idea where they're going. We are all guilty of describing the bride as looking lovely as she walked down the aisle. But that's not what she does. Any bride who comes gliding down the center of the church is not walking down the aisle. The middle passageway in a church is called the "nave," along with the pews on either side. It's the side passageways that are correctly called the "aisles." So how did we all get so turned around?

Old English is to blame. A word was used, spelled I-S-L-E, which meant "the surrounding area." When they talked about the "middle isle," they were referring to the whole center section of the church. Through time, "middle isle" became misunderstood as "middle aisle," and we've all been talking about the wrong thing since.

The bridegroom could care less about what aisle his bride is walking down as she comes to join him at the altar. He's proud, happy, excited, and thankful, and that's all he's aware of at that moment. If you know those feelings, then you know what joy there is in heaven when you choose to be a child of Jesus. The Bible describes it this way: "As a bridegroom rejoices over his bride, so will your God rejoice over you" (Isaiah 62:5, NIV). When you decide to join Jesus, you can be absolutely positive that he will be waiting to receive you with open arms.

# Why was a statue dedicated to a bug?

Things couldn't have been worse. In 1915 the farmers in Enterprise, Alabama, were losing one-third of their cotton crops, and all hope of planting more, to the insect called the Mexican boll weevil. With their livelihood all but destroyed, you would think that the town of Enterprise would never want to see another boll weevil again. Instead, three years later, they built a bronze statue honoring the boll weevil in the town square. Why?

Farmers realized that they could no longer depend on just one crop. After the boll weevil did its damage, there was a big change in the crops that were planted. Farmers began to diversify by growing corn, hay, potatoes, peanuts, and sugarcane. This led to prosperity for everyone and gratitude to the bug that started it all.

Nothing is too difficult for God. He can turn every bad thing into something good. He says, "I will give you back the crops the locusts ate!" (Joel 2:25). Whatever your hardship may be, never underestimate God!

# 193

# Why is the windchill colder than the air temperature?

When the weather gets near the freezing point, most of us begin to worry about wrapping up our water pipes so they won't burst. The weatherman who is announcing a windchill factor of minus 20 can make us extremely anxious about our car engines freezing. But before you grab those blankets, take a moment to understand what *windchill* really means.

The weatherman considers the actual temperature of the air and then adds in the wind. Wind will mean that the air feels colder, with *feels* being the word to emphasize. It is our skin that registers the "windchill factor." Nonliving objects can't feel, so they are never going to cool down to the chill factor. Objects will only get as cold as the actual temperature. When the weatherman tells you that the temperature is 35 degrees but the windchill is 15 degrees, interpret this news as "I'd better dress warmly enough to protect myself against coldness of 15 degrees because that's what the air will feel like. But because the temperature is 35 degrees, I won't have to worry about the pipes freezing unless the temperature actually drops below 32 degrees."

Keeping up with the weather is a hobby for many of us. We learn to cope with it because we certainly can't control it. That belongs only to God. The Bible says, "He sends his orders to the world. How swiftly his word flies. He sends the snow in all its lovely whiteness, scatters the frost upon the ground, and hurls the hail upon the earth. Who can stand before his freezing cold? But then he calls for warmer weather, and the spring winds blow and all the river ice is broken" (Psalm 147:15-18). Watching the weather is another way to marvel at God's wondrous world.

---

### 194

# Why were windshield wipers invented?

When rain or snow is blocking your vision through the windshield of your car, you push or pull a button, and the problem is wiped away. It wasn't always so easy. The trolley-car drivers in New York City in the early 1900s had to stop the trolley, leave their seats, step out into the bad weather, and wipe the windshield themselves. The worse the weather, the more often the trolley stopped, and the longer it took to travel anywhere.

One passenger, Mary Anderson, became impatient. She knew that the trolley drivers needed a way to clear the windshield from the inside so that they wouldn't have to keep stopping the trolley. Mary thought about their problem. She always washed her own windows by tying a sponge to the end of a stick and pushing it across the glass.

Mary wondered why the trolley drivers couldn't do the same thing. She experimented and finally found a long strip of hard rubber that could clear a windshield when tied to a pole. She fixed the pole to the windshield and connected it to the inside with a lever that the driver could move from his seat. The trolley driver who first tried the wiper in 1902 found that it worked beautifully. Mary Anderson started an idea that is now part of every bus, train, car, and plane.

You can ask God for a brand-new pair of "windshield wipers" that have nothing to do with auto parts. If you've been reading the Bible but feel you're not understanding the Scriptures as much as you'd like to, God can help. The Bible says, "The Lord gives sight to the blind" (Psalm 146:8, NIV). Ask God to make his Word clear to you, and he will.

# 195

# Why do we call them "wisdom teeth"?

Long ago people really needed their wisdom teeth. Meat was very chewy and tough, so the wisdom teeth helped people break it down. But over the centuries, the human jaw has gradually become shorter, so most people no longer have room in their mouth for those four back molars. Why the name "wisdom" teeth? These teeth don't try to come in until you're at least 18 years old, and you're *supposed* to be somewhat wise by then.

Being "wise" doesn't just mean being smart. It means that you have an understanding about what's important. The Bible clarifies for us what it really means to be wise: "Notice among yourselves, dear brothers, that few of you who follow Christ have big names or power or wealth. Instead, God has deliberately chosen to use ideas the world considers foolish and of little worth in order to shame those people considered by the world as wise and great. He has chosen a plan despised by the world, counted as nothing at all, and used it to bring down to nothing those the world considers great" (1 Corinthians 1:26-28). When you are truly wise in God's eyes, you understand that the most important part of your life is your belief in Jesus Christ. The wisest thing you can ever do is to ask Jesus to be your Lord.

# 196
# How did a lost cabby help save a life?

William Cowper lived in London in 1763. He had made up his mind that his life was hopeless and that the only way out was to commit suicide. He decided to jump off the bridge that spanned the Thames River and called a cab to take him there. After driving around, the cabdriver complained that the thick fog was making it impossible for him to figure out where they were. Not only couldn't he find the bridge, but he didn't even know how to take William home.

Out of frustration, the driver demanded that William get out of the cab immediately. William obeyed. When he looked around to get his bearings, he realized with amazement that he was standing in front of his own house! Gone were thoughts of suicide. Instead, William Cowper went into his house and wrote the famous hymn "God Moves in a Mysterious Way."

God has a way of protecting us, even when we're not aware of it. The Bible says, "He lifted me out of the pit of despair, out from the bog and the mire, and set my feet on a hard, firm path, and steadied me as I walked along. He has given me a new song to sing, of praises to our God" (Psalm 40:2-3). Whenever you're afraid that there is no more hope, turn toward God. He's been waiting for you.

## 197

# What were sheep doing at the White House?

There are a few things you may not know about sheep. In 1917 a small flock lived on the White House lawn. They were President Woodrow Wilson's idea so that the lawn could stay trimmed without using valuable manpower that was needed during World War I. When the sheep also ate some of the beautiful landscaping, like the bushes and flowers, on the White House lawn, people objected. But Mrs. Wilson pointed out that the sheep had also provided 98 pounds of wool that had been auctioned to make a contribution to the Red Cross.

Sheep are responsible for giving us the phrase about "knocking the tar" out of something. Long ago, when sheep received accidental cuts during shearing, tar was smeared on the wound. This helped to prevent infection, but it also made a mess by sticking to the wool. Before the wool could be sold, the shearer had to "knock the tar" out of it.

Another interesting fact about sheep is that they are afraid to drink from running water. It doesn't seem reasonable for sheep to avoid a flowing stream when they're thirsty. Remember, though, that some of our fears aren't rational, either. God understands our vulnerability. He wants to meet us where we are and escort us to a stronger place. He knows your deepest fears and understands that they bother you. He wants to help you to become more trusting of his protection. He will do this in a gentle way if you'll only allow him to. Think of Jesus as a shepherd and yourself as one of those frightened sheep.

The Bible tells how Jesus will take care of you. It says, "Because the Lord is my Shepherd, I have everything I need! He lets me rest in the meadow grass and leads me beside the quiet streams. He gives me new strength. He helps me do what honors him the most. Even when walking through the dark valley of death I will not be afraid, for you are close beside me, guarding, guiding all the way" (Psalm 23:1-4). If

Jesus is so sensitive to, and will take such good care of, an animal, imagine how much more precious you are to him. Let him lead you to quiet waters in your soul so that you can enjoy the refreshment.

## 198

# What does the *X* in *Xmas* stand for?

Around Christmastime you have probably noticed signs that say "Xmas" instead of Christmas. Maybe you thought that in our hustle-bustle world, the word was written that way to make it shorter and faster to read and write. Or maybe you thought that people were trying to leave Christ out of Christmas completely. But neither of those reasons are truly why the *X* is used. Actually, Christians themselves first started using the *X* long ago in Greece. The Greek letter for the beginning of Christ's name is *chi*, and the way to write *chi* is with an *X*. The *X* is just an old way of using Christ's initial.

The letter *X* is the symbol for Christ, who is the symbol of all beginnings. The Bible says, "Before anything else existed, there was Christ, with God. He has always been alive and is himself God. He created everything there is—nothing exists that he didn't make" (John 1:1-3). If you haven't already asked Jesus to begin his work in you, why not do so today? He will give you a whole new life.

# Why are cowards considered yellow?

To trace the cowardly meaning for the color yellow, you have to go back before the Civil War. Slavery was dividing the country. People both for and against slavery began publishing unsigned pamphlets that criticized well-known people. These lies and false accusations were written on inexpensive yellowish paper.

Because no one would stand behind the criticisms by signing their names, the yellow pamphlets were considered cowardly. After people found out that even newspaper editors were involved in the slandering, the term *yellow journalism* started being used. Finally, yellow was used to represent anything that a coward might do.

Fear is a powerful opponent but not more powerful than God. When you are afraid, you should realize that fear does not come from God. The Bible tells us, "The Holy Spirit, God's gift, does not want you to be afraid of people, but to be wise and strong, and to love them and enjoy being with them" (2 Timothy 1:7). If fear follows you, ask God to intervene. He will give you his peace and protection.

# What were deeds doing in cereal boxes?

In 1955 you could become a landowner each time you opened a box of cereal. That's because the Quaker Oats Company tucked a free deed of sale in each box of Puffed Rice and Puffed Wheat. The only catch was that the land you just acquired was exactly one square inch. This unusual idea was part of a unique marketing scheme.

Quaker Oats was sponsoring a television show for children: *Sergeant Preston of the Yukon.* So they arranged to buy 19.11 acres of the Yukon Territory from Canada. After the land was divided, 21 million numbered deeds were put into cereal boxes. Only one person actually tried to claim the property. He said that he had collected enough certificates to be the owner of a 75-square-foot plot. Quaker Oats checked but found that his pieces of land weren't next to each other. In the end, the land was reclaimed by Canada, and all that remained was the memory of a "mini" media masterpiece.

With the exception of the one man, everyone understood that their Yukon property was just for fun, just part of an interesting promotion. When it comes to the real property in our life, we sometimes get caught up in "ownership," being proud to say that the yard or the block or the thousand acres "belong" to us. Technically, you may have bought it from someone else, and in the eyes of the law, it's yours. But it was mere humans who made the laws, and mere humans who conducted the transfers. The fact is, we didn't make the land. Ultimately it belongs to someone else.

The Bible says, "The earth belongs to God! Everything in all the world is his! He is the one who pushed the oceans back to let dry land appear" (Psalm 24:1-2). We are only entitled to use the land because of God's generosity, in much the same way that you would loan a book to a friend and tell him to keep it as long as he'd like. During the time that he used the book, you would expect him to treat it with respect because it really belongs to you. If you own land, remember to appreciate it as the blessing God intended it to be.

# BIBLIOGRAPHY ━━━━━━━━━━━━━━━━━━━━━

**1. How did those sneakers get such a strange name?**
Smith, Douglas B. *More Ever Wonder Why?* New York: Ballantine Books, 1994.

**2. When can age be deceiving?**
Sobol, Donald J. *Encyclopedia Brown's Second Record Book of Weird and Wonderful Facts.* New York: Delacorte Press, 1981.
————. *Encyclopedia Brown's Third Record Book of Weird and Wonderful Facts.* New York: William Morrow and Co., 1985.

**3. When is your gas tank most dangerous?**
Burnam, Tom. *The Dictionary of Misinformation.* New York: Ballantine Books, 1975.

**4. Why didn't Americans want to change their currency?**
Flexner, Stuart Berg. *Listening to America.* New York: Simon and Schuster, 1982.
Goldberg, M. Hirsh. *The Blunder Book.* New York: William Morrow and Co., 1984.

**5. Why were people with a headache advised to chew a tree?**
Boyd, L. M. *Boyd's Book of Odd Facts.* New York: Sterling Publishing, 1979.
Felder, Deborah G. *The Kids' World Almanac of History.* New York: Pharos Books, 1991.
Giscard d'Estaing, Valerie-Anne. *Inventions.* New York: World Almanac Publications, 1985.
Harris, Harry. *Good Old-Fashioned Yankee Ingenuity.* Chelsea, Mich.: Scarborough House, 1990.
Jones, Charlotte Foltz. *Mistakes That Worked.* New York: Doubleday, 1991.
Panati, Charles. *The Browser's Book of Beginnings.* Boston: Houghton Mifflin, 1984.
————. *Panati's Extraordinary Origins of Everyday Things.* New York: Harper and Row, 1987.

Perko, Marko. *Did You Know That . . . ?* New York: Berkley Books, 1994.

Robertson, Patrick. *The Book of Firsts.* New York: Bramhall House, 1974.

Rovin, Jeff. *The Unbelievable Truth!* New York: Signet, 1994.

## 6. When can you buy an antique by scratching your nose?

Polley, Jane, ed. *Stories behind Everyday Things.* New York: Reader's Digest Association, 1980.

## 7. When can a backlog be helpful?

Claiborne, Robert. *Loose Cannons and Red Herrings.* New York: W. W. Norton and Co., 1988.

## 8. When do you let the "cat out of the bag"?

Claiborne, Robert. *Loose Cannons and Red Herrings.* New York: W. W. Norton and Co., 1988.

Funk, Charles Earle. *A Hog on Ice and Other Curious Expressions.* New York: Harper and Row, 1948.

McLoone, Margo, and Alice Siegel. *The Second Kids' World Almanac of Records and Facts.* New York: World Almanac Publications, 1987.

Morris, William, and Mary Morris. *Morris Dictionary of Word and Phrase Origins.* 2d ed. New York: HarperCollins, 1988.

Paisner, Milton. *One Word Leads to Another: A Light History of Words.* New York: Dembner Books, 1982.

Smith, Douglas B. *Ever Wonder Why?* New York: Ballantine Books, 1991.

Vanoni, Marvin. *Great Expressions.* New York: William Morrow and Co., 1989.

## 9. How did a bathtub help solve a mystery?

Clements, Gillian. *The Picture History of Great Inventors.* New York: Alfred A. Knopf, 1994.

Giscard d'Estaing, Valerie-Anne. *Inventions.* New York: World Almanac Publications, 1985.

Goodenough, Simon. *1500 Fascinating Facts.* London: Treasure Press, 1987.

## 10. How did cowboys carry their meals?

Flexner, Stuart Berg. *Listening to America.* New York: Simon and Schuster, 1982.

Sanders, Deidre, et al. *Would You Believe This, Too?* New York: Sterling Publishing, 1976.

Smith, Douglas B. *Ever Wonder Why?* New York: Ballantine Books, 1991.

## 11. Why are men's and women's bikes different?

Feldman, David. *Why Do Clocks Run Clockwise? and Other Imponderables.* New York: Harper and Row, 1987.

Lurie, Susan, ed. *The Big Book of Amazing Knowledge.* New York: Playmore, Inc., 1987.

McCutcheon, Marc. *The Writer's Guide to Everyday Life in the 1800s.* Cincinnati, Ohio: Writer's Digest Books, 1993.

## 12. Why do birds fly in a V formation?

Robbins, Pat, ed. *Why in the World?* Washington, D.C.: National Geographic Society, 1985.

Smith, Douglas B. *Ever Wonder Why?* New York: Ballantine Books, 1991.

## 13. How did a dead fish help frozen foods flourish?

Aaseng, Nathan. *The Rejects.* Minneapolis: Lerner Publications, 1989.

Buchman, Dian Dincin, and Seli Groves. *What If? Fifty Discoveries That Changed the World.* New York: Scholastic, Inc., 1988.

Campbell, Hannah. *Why Did They Name It . . . ?* New York: Fleet Publishing, 1964.

Fabell, Walter C. *Nature's Clues.* New York: Hastings House, 1964.

Flexner, Stuart Berg. *Listening to America.* New York: Simon and Schuster, 1982.

Giscard d'Estaing, Valerie-Anne. *Inventions.* New York: World Almanac Publications, 1985.

Landau, Irwin, ed. *I'll Buy That.* New York: Consumer Reports, 1986.

Montague, Ashley, and Edward Darling. *The Prevalence of Nonsense.* New York: Harper and Row, 1967.

Perko, Marko. *Did You Know That . . . ?* New York: Berkley Books, 1994.

Polley, Jane, ed. *Stories behind Everyday Things.* New York: Reader's Digest Association, 1980.

Robertson, Patrick. *The Book of Firsts.* New York: Bramhall House, 1974.

Sanders, Deidre, et al. *Would You Believe This, Too?* New York: Sterling Publishing, 1976.

## 14. When can books become a bother?

*Reader's Digest Facts and Fallacies.* New York: Reader's Digest Association, 1988.

## 15. How did a medicine bottle turn into a toy?

Schreiber, Brad. *Weird Wonders and Bizarre Blunders.* New York: Simon and Schuster, 1989.

**16. Which church leader picked nine pins for bowling?**

Elwood, Ann, and Carol Orsag. *Macmillan Illustrated Almanac for Kids.* New York: Macmillan, 1981.

Giscard d'Estaing, Valerie-Anne. *Inventions.* New York: World Almanac Publications, 1985.

McCutcheon, Marc. *The Writer's Guide to Everyday Life in the 1800s.* Cincinnati, Ohio: Writer's Digest Books, 1993.

Morris, Scot. *The Emperor Who Ate the Bible and More Strange Facts and Useless Information.* New York: Doubleday, 1991.

Smith, Douglas B. *More Ever Wonder Why?* New York: Ballantine Books, 1994.

Wallechinsky, David, and Irving Wallace. *The People's Almanac Presents the Book of Lists 2.* New York: Bantam Books, 1978.

Wulffson, Don L. *How Sports Came to Be.* New York: Lothrop, Lee, and Shepard, 1980.

**17. How could treason be committed during dinner?**

Morris, Scot. *The Emperor Who Ate the Bible and More Strange Facts and Useless Information.* New York: Doubleday, 1991.

**18. What causes bad breath?**

Editors of *Owl* magazine. *The Kids' Question and Answer Book Three.* New York: Grosset and Dunlap, 1990.

Feldman, David. *Why Do Dogs Have Wet Noses? and Other Imponderables.* New York: HarperCollins, 1990.

Murphy, Jim. *Guess Again: More Weird and Wacky Inventions.* New York: Bradbury Press, 1986.

Rovin, Jeff. *The Unbelievable Truth!* New York: The Penguin Group, 1994.

Varasdi, J. Allen. *Myth Information.* New York: Ballantine Books, 1989.

**19. Why would two brothers booby-trap their house?**

*Reader's Digest Facts and Fallacies.* New York: Reader's Digest Association, 1988.

Smith, Richard, and Edward Decter. *Oops! The Complete Book of Bloopers.* New York: The Rutledge Press, 1981.

**20. What's up with eyebrows?**

Tuleja, Tad. *Curious Customs.* New York: Stonesong Press, 1987.

**21. How do you build a skyscraper with matchsticks?**

Buchman, Dian Dincin, and Seli Groves. *What If? Fifty Discoveries That Changed the World.* New York: Scholastic, Inc., 1988.

Burnam, Tom. *The Dictionary of Misinformation*. New York: Ballantine Books, 1975.

Harris, Harry. *Good Old-Fashioned Yankee Ingenuity*. Chelsea, Mich.: Scarborough House, 1990.

Meyers, James. *Amazing Facts*. New York: Playmore, Inc., 1986.

**22. What really makes a bull charge at a red cape?**

Blumberg, Rhoda, and Leda Blumberg. *The Simon and Schuster Book of Facts and Fallacies*. New York: Simon and Schuster, 1983.

Burnam, Tom. *The Dictionary of Misinformation*. New York: Ballantine Books, 1975.

McLoone, Margo, and Alice Siegel. *The Second Kids' World Almanac of Records and Facts*. New York: World Almanac Publications, 1987.

Meyers, James. *Amazing Facts*. New York: Playmore, Inc., 1986.

Perko, Marko. *Did You Know That . . . ?* New York: Berkley Books, 1994.

Simon, Seymour. *Animal Fact, Animal Fable*. New York: Crown Publishing, 1979.

Smith, Douglas B. *Ever Wonder Why?* New York: Ballantine Books, 1991.

Tuleja, Ted. *Fabulous Fallacies*. South Yarmouth, Mass.: John Curley and Associates, Inc., 1982.

Varasdi, J. Allen. *Myth Information*. New York: Ballantine Books, 1989.

**23. How did a Christmas card lead to a unique advertising campaign?**

Campbell, Hannah. *Why Did They Name It . . . ?* New York: Fleet Publishing, 1964.

Flexner, Stuart Berg. *Listening to America*. New York: Simon and Schuster, 1982.

Morgan, Hal. *Symbols of America*. New York: Viking, 1986.

Rowesome, Frank Jr. *The Verse by the Side of the Road*. Brattleboro, Vt.: Stephen Greene Press, 1965.

Wallechinsky, David, and Irving Wallace. *The People's Almanac*. New York: Doubleday, 1975.

**24. What can you do with a useless tunnel?**

Wallace, Irving, Amy Wallace, and David Wallechinsky. *Significa*. New York: E. P. Dutton, Inc., 1983.

**25. Why leave your business card when you don't even work?**

Perko, Marko. *Did You Know That . . . ?* New York: Berkley Books, 1994.

Tuleja, Tad. *Curious Customs*. New York: Stonesong Press, 1987.

**26. How did a tomato create an emergency by calling 9-1-1?**
Felton, Bruce. *One of a Kind*. New York: William Morrow and Co., 1992.

**27. What can you do with a pack of camels?**
Felton, Bruce. *One of a Kind*. New York: William Morrow and Co., 1992.
Felton, Bruce, and Mark Fowler. *Felton and Fowler's Best, Worst, and Most Unusual*. New York: Thomas Y. Crowell, 1975.
Lurie, Susan, ed. *The Big Book of Amazing Knowledge*. New York: Playmore, Inc., 1987.
Morris, Scot. *The Emperor Who Ate the Bible and More Strange Facts and Useless Information*. New York: Doubleday, 1991.
Perl, Lila. *It Happened in America*. New York: Henry Holt and Co., 1992.
Vogel, Malvina G., ed. *The Big Book of Amazing Facts*. New York: Playmore, Inc., 1980.

**28. How were Life Savers saved?**
Campbell, Hannah. *Why Did They Name It . . . ?* New York: Fleet Publishing, 1964.
Caney, Steven. *Steven Caney's Invention Book*. New York: Workman Publishing, 1985.
Harris, Harry. *Good Old-Fashioned Yankee Ingenuity*. Chelsea, Mich.: Scarborough House, 1990.

**29. Why are a cat's whiskers better than a man's?**
Louis, David. *2201 Fascinating Facts*. New York: Crown Publishing, 1983.
Squire, Dr. Ann. *101 Questions and Answers about Pets and People*. New York: Macmillan, 1988.

**30. Why do all movie scenes start with that black-and-white clapboard?**
Smith, Douglas B. *More Ever Wonder Why?* New York: Ballantine Books, 1994.

**31. When can colors be confusing?**
Goldwyn, Martin M. *How a Fly Walks Upside Down . . . and Other Curious Facts*. New York: Carol Publishing, 1979.
Meyers, James. *Amazing Facts*. New York: Playmore, Inc., 1986.
———. *The Best Amazing Question and Answer Book*. New York: Playmore, Inc., 1987.
Vogel, Malvina G., ed. *The Big Book of Amazing Facts*. New York: Playmore, Inc., 1980.

**32. Why did some coffins have alarms?**
Felton, Bruce. *One of a Kind*. New York: William Morrow and Co., 1992.

Felton, Bruce, and Mark Fowler. *Felton and Fowler's More Best, Worst, and Most Unusual.* New York: Fawcett Crest, 1976.

McCutcheon, Marc. *The Writer's Guide to Everyday Life in the 1800s.* Cincinnati, Ohio: Writer's Digest Books, 1993.

Varasdi, J. Allen. *Myth Information.* New York: Ballantine Books, 1989.

### 33. How did clay flowerpots help make buildings better?

Harvey, Edmund, ed. *Reader's Digest Book of Facts.* New York: Reader's Digest Association, 1987.

### 34. What did a touch tell in trial?

Felton, Bruce, and Mark Fowler. *Felton and Fowler's Best, Worst, and Most Unusual.* New York: Thomas Y. Crowell, 1975.

Fullerton, Timothy T. *Triviata: A Compendium of Useless Information.* New York: Hart Publishing, 1975.

### 35. What's the big secret behind Betty Crocker?

Boyd, L. M. *Boyd's Book of Odd Facts.* New York: Sterling Publishing, 1979.

Campbell, Hannah. *Why Did They Name It . . . ?* New York: Fleet Publishing, 1964.

Morgan, Hal. *Symbols of America.* New York: Viking, 1986.

Panati, Charles. *Panati's Extraordinary Origins of Everyday Things.* New York: Harper and Row, 1987.

Tuleja, Tad. *The New York Public Library Book of Popular Americana.* New York: Macmillan, 1994.

Varasdi, J. Allen. *Myth Information.* New York: Ballantine Books, 1989.

### 36. What sent the price of raccoon tails climbing?

Asakawa, Gil, and Leland Rucker. *The Toy Book.* New York: Alfred A. Knopf, 1992.

Panati, Charles. *Panati's Parade of Fads, Follies, and Manias.* New York: HarperCollins, 1991.

### 37. How are crossword puzzles connected with Christmas?

Burnam, Tom. *The Dictionary of Misinformation.* New York: Ballantine Books, 1975.

Giscard d'Estaing, Valerie-Anne. *Inventions.* New York: World Almanac Publications, 1985.

Harris, Harry. *Good Old-Fashioned Yankee Ingenuity.* Chelsea, Mich.: Scarborough House, 1990.

King, Norman. *The Almanac of Fascinating Beginnings.* New York: Carol Publishing, 1994.

Lurie, Susan, ed. *The Big Book of Amazing Knowledge.* New York: Playmore, Inc., 1987.

Panati, Charles. *Panati's Parade of Fads, Follies, and Manias.* New York: HarperCollins, 1991.

Robertson, Patrick. *The Book of Firsts.* New York: Bramhall House, 1974.

## 38. Why did farmers have curfews?

Ayto, John. *Dictionary of Word Origins.* New York: Arcade Publishing, 1990.

Claiborne, Robert. *Loose Cannons and Red Herrings.* New York: W. W. Norton and Co., 1988.

Justice, Dr. David B., ed. *Webster's Word Histories.* Springfield, Mass.: Merriam-Webster, Inc., 1989.

Muschell, David. *Where in the Word?* Roseville, Calif.: Prima Publishing, 1990.

Soukhanov, Anne H., ed. *Word Mysteries and Histories.* Boston: Houghton Mifflin, 1986.

Vanoni, Marvin. *Great Expressions.* New York: William Morrow and Co., 1989.

## 39. Where were houses built roof-first and books read back to front?

Leokum, Arkady. *The Curious Book.* New York: Sterling Publishing, 1976.

Louis, David. *2201 Fascinating Facts.* New York: Crown Publishing, 1983.

## 40. Why did a priest decide to live with lepers?

McLoughlin, E. V., ed. *The Book of Knowledge.* Vol. 7. New York: The Grolier Society, Inc., 1946.

Varasdi, J. Allen. *Myth Information.* New York: Ballantine Books, 1989.

## 41. Who served as president for only one day?

Lurie, Susan, ed. *The Big Book of Amazing Knowledge.* New York: Playmore, Inc., 1987.

Perko, Marko. *Did You Know That . . . ?* New York: Berkley Books, 1994.

Vogel, Malvina G., ed. *The Big Book of Amazing Facts.* New York: Playmore, Inc., 1980.

## 42. Which author was always tempted by risky investments?

Publishers of *Yankee Magazine. The Inventive Yankee.* Dublin, N.H.: Yankee Books, 1989.

## 43. When can you strike a nerve at the dentist's office?

Burnam, Tom. *The Dictionary of Misinformation.* New York: Ballantine Books, 1975.

### 44. Where does dew come from if it doesn't fall?
Burnam, Tom. *More Misinformation*. New York: Ballantine Books, 1980.
Goldwyn, Martin M. *How a Fly Walks Upside Down . . . and Other Curious Facts*. New York: Carol Publishing, 1979.
Varasdi, J. Allen. *Myth Information*. New York: Ballantine Books, 1989.

### 45. What's the spin on revolving doors?
Zotti, Ed. *Know It All!* New York: Ballantine Books, 1993.

### 46. How did the tuxedo get its name?
Harris, Harry. *Good Old-Fashioned Yankee Ingenuity*. Chelsea, Mich.: Scarborough House, 1990.
Limburg, Peter R. *Stories behind Words*. New York: H. W. Wilson, 1986.
Rovin, Jeff. *The Unbelievable Truth!* New York: The Penguin Group, 1994.
Smith, Douglas B. *More Ever Wonder Why?* New York: Ballantine Books, 1994.

### 47. Why do we drive on the right side of the road?
McCutcheon, Marc. *The Writer's Guide to Everyday Life in the 1800s*. Cincinnati, Ohio: Writer's Digest Books, 1993.
Smith, Douglas B. *Ever Wonder Why?* New York: Ballantine Books, 1991.
Tuleja, Tad. *Curious Customs*. New York: Stonesong Press, 1987.
Vogel, Malvina G., ed. *The Big Book of Amazing Facts*. New York: Playmore, Inc., 1980.

### 48. Why does laundry get wet when it's dry-cleaned?
Giscard d'Estaing, Valerie-Anne. *Inventions*. New York: World Almanac Publications, 1985.
Rovin, Jeff. *The Unbelievable Truth!* New York: The Penguin Group, 1994.
Sutton, Caroline. *How Do They Do That?* New York: Quill, 1982.
Sutton, Caroline, and Kevin Markey. *More How Do They Do That?* New York: William Morrow and Co., 1993.

### 49. How did a brilliant man's name develop into "dunce"?
Perko, Marko. *Did You Know That . . . ?* New York: Berkley Books, 1994.
Smith, Douglas B. *Ever Wonder Why?* New York: Ballantine Books, 1991.
Wallace, Irving, Amy Wallace, and David Wallechinsky. *Significa*. New York: E. P. Dutton, Inc., 1983.

### 50. Why did the Dutch build a memorial for a fictional character?
Morris, Scot. *The Emperor Who Ate the Bible and More Strange Facts and Useless Information*. New York: Doubleday, 1991.

Tuleja, Tad. *Fabulous Fallacies.* South Yarmouth, Mass.: John Curley and Associates, Inc., 1982.

**51. Why isn't the bald eagle bald?**
Perko, Marko. *Did You Know That . . . ?* New York: Berkley Books, 1994.
Smith, Douglas B. *More Ever Wonder Why?* New York: Ballantine Books, 1994.
Varasdi, J. Allen. *Myth Information.* New York: Ballantine Books, 1989.
Vogel, Malvina G., ed. *The Big Book of Amazing Facts.* New York: Playmore, Inc., 1980.

**52. What do roofs and ears have in common?**
Editors of American Heritage Dictionaries. *Word Mysteries and Histories.* Boston: Houghton Mifflin, 1986.
Funk, Charles Earle. *Horsefeathers and Other Curious Words.* New York: Harper and Row, 1958.
Smith, Douglas B. *More Ever Wonder Why?* New York: Ballantine Books, 1994.

**53. Where did Thomas Edison go on vacation?**
Humes, James C. *Speaker's Treasury of Anecdotes about the Famous.* New York: Harper and Row, 1978.
Pim, Paul. *Telling Tommy about Famous Inventors.* New York: Cupples and Leon Co., 1942.
Thompson, C. E. *101 Wacky Facts about Kids.* New York: Scholastic, Inc., 1992.

**54. When was the United States ruled by an emperor?**
Felton, Bruce, and Mark Fowler. *Felton and Fowler's Best, Worst, and Most Unusual.* New York: Thomas Y. Crowell, 1975.
Lurie, Susan, ed. *A Treasury of Amazing Knowledge.* New York: Playmore, Inc., 1988.
Lyon, Ron, and Jenny Paschall. *Beyond Belief.* New York: Villard Books, 1993.
Urton, Andrea. *Now Entering Weirdsville!* Los Angeles: Lowell House Juvenile, 1992.

**55. How did some prisoners dig themselves into deeper trouble?**
Pile, Stephen. *The Book of Heroic Failures.* London: Routledge and Kegan Paul, Ltd., 1979.
Pringle, Laurence. *"The Earth Is Flat" and Other Great Mistakes.* New York: William Morrow and Co., 1983.

Smith, Richard, and Edward Decter. *Oops! The Complete Book of Bloopers.* New York: The Rutledge Press, 1981.

### 56. Why does one eye work harder than the other?
Vogel, Malvina G., ed. *The Big Book of Amazing Facts.* New York: Playmore, Inc., 1980.

### 57. Why doesn't a fan cool the air?
Burnam, Tom. *The Dictionary of Misinformation.* New York: Ballantine Books, 1975.

Rosenbloom, Joseph. *Bananas Don't Grow on Trees: A Guide to Popular Misconceptions.* New York: Sterling Publishing, 1978.

Rovin, Jeff. *The Unbelievable Truth!* New York: The Penguin Group, 1994.

Vogel, Malvina G., ed. *The Big Book of Amazing Facts.* New York: Playmore, Inc., 1980.

### 58. When did paying a library fine make history?
Lee, Stan. *Stan Lee Presents the Best of the Worst.* New York: Harper and Row, 1979.

Pile, Stephen. *The Book of Heroic Failures.* London: Routledge and Kegan Paul, Ltd., 1979.

### 59. What plant only grows after being burned by a fire?
Harvey, Edmund, ed. *Reader's Digest Book of Facts.* New York: Reader's Digest Association, 1987.

### 60. How did the meaning of a flag at half-mast change?
Rovin, Jeff. *The Unbelievable Truth!* New York: The Penguin Group, 1994.

Smith, Douglas B. *Ever Wonder Why?* New York: Ballantine Books, 1991.

Tuleja, Tad. *Curious Customs.* New York: Stonesong Press, 1987.

### 61. Why aren't there any fleas at a flea market?
Smith, Douglas B. *More Ever Wonder Why?* New York: Ballantine Books, 1994.

### 62. Are you seeing things?
Zotti, Ed. *Know It All!* New York: Ballantine Books, 1993.

### 63. Which flower looks like a lion's teeth?
Editors of American Heritage Dictionaries. *Word Mysteries and Histories.* Boston: Houghton Mifflin, 1986.

Muschell, David. *Where in the Word?* Roseville, Calif.: Prima Publishing, 1990.

**64. Who used fingerprints to make a contract binding?**
Blumberg, Rhoda, and Leda Blumberg. *The Simon and Schuster Book of Facts and Fallacies*. New York: Simon and Schuster, 1983.
Fabell, Walter C. *Nature's Clues*. New York: Hastings House, 1964.
Lurie, Susan, ed. *The Big Book of Amazing Knowledge*. New York: Playmore, Inc., 1987.
Robertson, Patrick. *The Book of Firsts*. New York: Bramhall House, 1974.
Rosenbloom, Joseph. *Polar Bears Like It Hot*. New York: Sterling Publishing, 1980.

**65. Why did W. C. Fields open so many bank accounts?**
Wallace, Irving, Amy Wallace, and David Wallechinsky. *Significa*. New York: E. P. Dutton, Inc., 1983.

**66. What is the five-year frog?**
Harvey, Edmund, ed. *Reader's Digest Book of Facts*. New York: Reader's Digest Association, 1987.

**67. Why was the general always absent during roll call?**
Wallace, Irving, Amy Wallace, and David Wallechinsky. *Significa*. New York: E. P. Dutton, Inc., 1983.

**68. When did spaghetti grow on trees?**
*Reader's Digest Facts and Fallacies*. New York: Reader's Digest Association, 1988.

**69. What did gloves say about hands?**
Polley, Jane, ed. *Stories behind Everyday Things*. New York: Reader's Digest Association, 1980.

**70. How did riches escape the man who started a gold rush?**
Harvey, Edmund, ed. *Reader's Digest Book of Facts*. New York: Reader's Digest Association, 1987.

**71. Why don't we eat goldfish?**
Panati, Charles. *The Browser's Book of Beginnings*. Boston: Houghton Mifflin, 1984.

**72. How did golf courses end up with 18 holes?**
Feldman, David. *Why Do Clocks Run Clockwise? and Other Imponderables*. New York: Harper and Row, 1987.
Perko, Marko. *Did You Know That . . . ?* New York: Berkley Books, 1994.
Phillips, Louis. *A Kids' Book of Lists: The World By Sevens*. New York: Franklin Watts, 1981.

Smith, Douglas B. *Ever Wonder Why?* New York: Ballantine Books, 1991.

**73. How did a fruit foul up a publicity stunt?**
Felton, Bruce. *One of a Kind.* New York: William Morrow and Co., 1992.

**74. What causes gray hair?**
Alway, Carol, et al. *Strange Stories, Amazing Facts.* New York: Reader's Digest Association, 1976.

Montague, Ashley, and Edward Darling. *The Prevalance of Nonsense.* New York: Harper and Row, 1967.

Rovin, Jeff. *The Unbelievable Truth!* New York: The Penguin Group, 1994.

Smith, Douglas B. *Ever Wonder Why?* New York: Ballantine Books, 1991.

Varasdi, J. Allen. *Myth Information.* New York: Ballantine Books, 1989.

Vogel, Malvina G., ed. *The Big Book of Amazing Facts.* New York: Playmore, Inc., 1980.

**75. Why are two security guards hired to stare up all day?**
Lee, Stan. *Stan Lee Presents the Best of the Worst.* New York: Harper and Row, 1979.

Louis, David. *2201 Fascinating Facts.* New York: Crown Publishing, 1983.

Pringle, Laurence. *"The Earth Is Flat" and Other Great Mistakes.* New York: William Morrow and Co., 1983.

Smith, Richard, and Edward Decter. *Oops! The Complete Book of Bloopers.* New York: The Rutledge Press, 1981.

**76. What are some predictable differences in people's hands?**
Louis, David. *2201 Fascinating Facts.* New York: Crown Publishing, 1983.

Rovin, Jeff. *The Unbelievable Truth!* New York: The Penguin Group, 1994.

Sobol, Donald J. *Encyclopedia Brown's Third Record Book of Weird and Wonderful Facts.* New York: William Morrow and Co., 1985.

**77. When was Hollywood a happy little hamlet?**
Flexner, Stuart Berg. *Listening to America.* New York: Simon and Schuster, 1982.

Harris, Harry. *Good Old-Fashioned Yankee Ingenuity.* Chelsea, Mich.: Scarborough House, 1990.

Louis, David. *2201 Fascinating Facts.* New York: Crown Publishing, 1983.

Smith, Douglas B. *More Ever Wonder Why?* New York: Ballantine Books, 1994.

Varasdi, J. Allen. *Myth Information.* New York: Ballantine Books, 1989.

Watkins, T. H. *California, An Illustrated History.* Palo Alto, Calif.: American West Publishing Co., 1973.

### 78. Why doesn't humble pie taste good?

Alway, Carol, et al. *Strange Stories, Amazing Facts.* New York: Reader's Digest Association, 1976.

Burnam, Tom. *The Dictionary of Misinformation.* New York: Ballantine Books, 1975.

Limburg, Peter R. *Stories behind Words.* New York: H. W. Wilson, 1986.

Smith, Douglas B. *Ever Wonder Why?* New York: Ballantine Books, 1991.

### 79. Which artist always depicted children but never had any?

Aaseng, Nathan. *The Unsung Heroes.* Minneapolis: Lerner Publications, 1989.

Panati, Charles. *Panati's Parade of Fads, Follies, and Manias.* New York: HarperCollins, 1991.

### 80. How can you get to sleep without counting sheep?

Boyd, L. M. *Boyd's Book of Odd Facts.* New York: Sterling Publishing, 1979.

Florman, Monte. *1,001 Helpful Tips, Facts, and Hints from Consumer Reports.* Mount Vernon, N.Y.: Consumers Union of U.S., Inc., 1989.

### 81. What do the letters IOU mean?

Boyd, L. M. *Boyd's Book of Odd Facts.* New York: Sterling Publishing, 1979.

Varasdi, J. Allen. *Myth Information.* New York: Ballantine Books, 1989.

### 82. Why has ironing always been a chore?

Felder, Deborah G. *The Kids' World Almanac of History.* New York: Pharos Books, 1991.

Panati, Charles. *Panati's Extraordinary Origins of Everyday Things.* New York: Harper and Row, 1987.

### 83. Who listened to Mozart and Shakespeare while stranded on a desert island?

McCormick, Donald. *The Master Book of Escapes.* New York: Franklin Watts, Inc., 1975.

### 84. How did the Jacuzzi get its name?

Harris, Harry. *Good Old-Fashioned Yankee Ingenuity.* Chelsea, Mich.: Scarborough House, 1990.

*Reader's Digest Facts and Fallacies.* New York: Reader's Digest Association, 1988.

### 85. How did the Jeep get its name?

Alway, Carol, et al. *Strange Stories, Amazing Facts.* New York: Reader's Digest Association, 1976.

Caney, Steven. *Steven Caney's Invention Book*. New York: Workman Publishing, 1985.

Epstein, Sam, and Beryl Epstein. *What's behind the Word?* New York: Scholastic Book Services, 1964.

Guttmacher, Peter. *Jeep*. New York: Macmillan, 1994.

Harris, Harry. *Good Old-Fashioned Yankee Ingenuity*. Chelsea, Mich.: Scarborough House, 1990.

Landau, Irwin, ed. *I'll Buy That*. New York: Consumers Union, 1986.

Lurie, Susan, ed. *A Treasury of Amazing Knowledge*. New York: Playmore, Inc., 1988.

Patton, Philippians. *Made in U.S.A.: The Secret Histories of the Things That Made America*. New York: Grove/Atlantic Monthly, 1992.

Robertson, Patrick. *The Book of Firsts*. New York: Bramhall House, 1974.

Smith, David, and Sue Cassin. *The Amazing Book of Firsts*. London: Victoria House Publishing, Ltd., 1990.

Smith, Douglas B. *Ever Wonder Why?* New York: Ballantine Books, 1991.

## 86. When did a painting turn into a puzzle?

Louis, David. *2201 Fascinating Facts*. New York: Crown Publishing, 1983.

## 87. How did marketing make Kleenex successful?

Caney, Steven. *Steven Caney's Invention Book*. New York: Workman Publishing, 1985.

Giscard d'Estaing, Valerie-Anne. *Inventions*. New York: World Almanac Publications, 1985.

King, Norman. *The Almanac of Fascinating Beginnings*. New York: Citadel Press, 1994.

Panati, Charles. *Panati's Extraordinary Origins of Everyday Things*. New York: Harper and Row, 1987.

Wallace, Irving, Amy Wallace, and David Wallechinsky. *Significa*. New York: E. P. Dutton, Inc., 1983.

## 88. How did a photographer's pictures change children's lives?

*Little Known and Famous Americans*. Columbus, Ohio: Essential Learning Products, 1992.

## 89. Is it possible to learn a language overnight?

Louis, David. *2201 Fascinating Facts*. New York: Crown Publishing, 1983.

Meyers, James. *The Best Amazing Question and Answer Book*. New York: Playmore, Inc., 1987.

**90. How do you address people with the same name?**

Caney, Steven. *Steven Caney's Kids' America*. New York: Workman Publishing, 1978.

Epstein, Sam, and Beryl Epstein. *What's behind the Word?* New York: Scholastic Book Services, 1964.

Flexner, Stuart Berg. *Listening to America*. New York: Simon and Schuster, 1982.

Goodenough, Simon. *1500 Fascinating Facts*. London: Treasure Press, 1987.

Smith, Douglas B. *More Ever Wonder Why?* New York: Ballantine Books, 1994.

Vogel, Malvina G., ed. *The Big Book of Amazing Facts*. New York: Playmore, Inc., 1980.

**91. How could you commit a crime with a pillow?**

Smith, Douglas B. *Ever Wonder Why?* New York: Ballantine Books, 1991.

**92. What's so great about grass?**

Felder, Deborah G. *The Kids' World Almanac of History*. New York: Pharos Books, 1991.

Feldman, David. *Why Do Clocks Run Clockwise? and Other Imponderables*. New York: Harper and Row, 1987.

Giscard d'Estaing, Valerie-Anne. *Inventions*. New York: World Almanac Publications, 1985.

Goldwyn, Martin M. *How a Fly Walks Upside Down . . . and Other Curious Facts*. New York: Carol Publishing, 1979.

Panati, Charles. *Panati's Extraordinary Origins of Everyday Things*. New York: Harper and Row, 1987.

———. *Panati's Parade of Fads, Follies, and Manias*. New York: HarperCollins, 1991.

Tuleja, Tad. *Curious Customs*. New York: Stonesong Press, 1987.

**93. What lieutenant wouldn't stop fighting World War II?**

Meyers, James. *Amazing Facts*. New York: Playmore, Inc., 1986.

Pile, Stephen. *The Book of Heroic Failures*. London: Routledge and Kegan Paul, Ltd., 1979.

Pringle, Laurence. *"The Earth Is Flat" and Other Great Mistakes*. New York: William Morrow and Co., 1983.

**94. Why did one letter take seven years to reach the White House?**

Sobol, Donald J. *Encyclopedia Brown's Second Record Book of Weird and Wonderful Facts*. New York: Delacorte Press, 1981.

**95. What did you get if you ordered "bossy in a bowl"?**

Choron, Sandra. *The Big Book of Kids' Lists.* New York: World Almanac Publications, 1985.

Flexner, Stuart Berg. *Listening to America.* New York: Simon and Schuster, Inc., 1982.

Panati, Charles. *Panati's Parade of Fads, Follies, and Manias.* New York: HarperCollins, 1991.

**96. What is the surprise ingredient in your cereal?**

Adams, Cecil. *Return of the Straight Dope.* New York: Ballantine Books, 1994.

Felton, Bruce. *One of a Kind.* New York: William Morrow and Co., 1992.

**97. When was delivering mail a challenge for mailmen?**

Schreiber, Brad. *Weird Wonders and Bizarre Blunders.* New York: Simon and Schuster, 1989.

Smith, Douglas B. *More Ever Wonder Why?* New York: Ballantine Books, 1994.

**98. What can happen if you only have one copy of your manuscript?**

Goodenough, Simon. *1500 Fascinating Facts.* London: Treasure Press, 1987.

Pile, Stephen. *The Book of Heroic Failures.* London: Routledge and Kegan Paul, Ltd., 1979.

Smith, Richard, and Edward Decter. *Oops! The Complete Book of Bloopers.* New York: The Rutledge Press, 1981.

**99. How did foot powder win a mayoral race?**

Felton, Bruce. *One of a Kind.* New York: William Morrow and Co., 1992.

Felton, Bruce, and Mark Fowler. *Felton and Fowler's More Best, Worst, and Most Unusual.* New York: Fawcett Crest, 1976.

Wullfson, Don L. *Amazing True Stories.* New York: Scholastic, Inc., 1991.

**100. Why would a house have 2,000 doors?**

Asimov, Isaac. *Would You Believe?* New York: Grossett and Dunlap, 1982.

Harvey, Edmund, ed. *Reader's Digest Book of Facts.* New York: Reader's Digest Association, 1987.

Manchester, Richard B. *Incredible Facts.* New York: Galahad Books, 1985.

Meyers, James. *The Best Amazing Question and Answer Book.* New York: Playmore, Inc., 1987.

**101. How did a nose and some fingertips help make measurements?**

Alway, Carol, et al. *Strange Stories, Amazing Facts.* New York: Reader's Digest Association, 1976.

Feldman, David. *Why Do Clocks Run Clockwise? and Other Imponderables.* New York: Harper and Row, 1987.

*How Things Change.* Chicago: Field Enterprises Educational Corporation, 1971.

Lurie, Susan, ed. *The Big Book of Amazing Knowledge.* New York: Playmore, Inc., 1987.

Panati, Charles. *The Browser's Book of Beginnings.* Boston: Houghton Mifflin, 1984.

Sanders, Deidre, et. al. *Would You Believe This, Too?* New York: Sterling Publishing, 1976.

Seuling, Barbara. *You Can't Sneeze with Your Eyes Open.* New York: E. P. Dutton, Inc., 1986.

Smith, Douglas B. *Ever Wonder Why?* New York: Ballantine Books, 1991.

Vogel, Malvina G., ed. *The Big Book of Amazing Facts.* New York: Playmore, Inc., 1980.

**102. Why does metal feel colder than wood?**

Ardley, Bridget, and Neil Ardley. *The Random House Book of 1001 Questions and Answers.* New York: Random House, 1989.

**103. What billion-dollar industry was created from paper cups and milk shakes?**

Aaseng, Nathan. *The Unsung Heroes.* Minneapolis: Lerner Publications, 1989.

Giscard d'Estaing, Valerie-Anne. *Inventions.* New York: World Almanac Publications, 1985.

Harris, Harry. *Good Old-Fashioned Yankee Ingenuity.* Chelsea, Mich.: Scarborough House, 1990.

Landau, Irwin, ed. *I'll Buy That.* New York: Consumers Union, 1986.

Meyers, James. *Eggplants, Elevators, Etc.: An Uncommon History of Common Things.* New York: Hart Publishing, 1978.

McLoone, Margo, and Alice Siegel. *The Kids' World Almanac of Records and Facts.* New York: World Almanac Publications, 1986.

Morgan, Hal. *Symbols of America.* New York: Viking, 1986.

Patton, Philippians. *Made in U.S.A.: The Secret Histories of the Things That Made America.* New York: Grove/Atlantic Monthly, 1992.

Sutton, Caroline. *How Did They Do That?* New York: William Morrow and Co., 1984.

Wallechinsky, David, and Irving Wallace. *The People's Almanac Presents the Book of Lists 2.* New York: Bantam Books, 1978.

### 104. What popular game began on the grounds of a motel?
Garrison, Webb. *Why Didn't I Think of That? From Alarm Clocks to Zippers.* Englewood Cliffs, N.J.: Prentice Hall, Inc., 1977.

Harris, Harry. *Good Old-Fashioned Yankee Ingenuity.* Chelsea, Mich.: Scarborough House, 1990.

Panati, Charles. *Panati's Parade of Fads, Follies, and Manias.* New York: HarperCollins, 1991.

### 105. Why did the richest woman in the world eat cold oatmeal?
Alway, Carol, et al. *Strange Stories, Amazing Facts.* New York: Reader's Digest Association, 1976.

Felder, Deborah G. *The Kids' World Almanac of History.* New York: Pharos Books, 1991.

Felton, Bruce, and Mark Fowler. *Felton and Fowler's Best, Worst, and Most Unusual.* New York: Thomas Y. Crowell, 1975.

McWhirter, Norris, and Ross McWhirter. *Guiness Book of Astounding Feats and Events.* New York: Sterling Publishing, 1975.

Morris, Scot. *The Emperor Who Ate the Bible and More Strange Facts and Useless Information.* New York: Doubleday, 1991.

Publishers of *Yankee Magazine. The Inventive Yankee.* Dublin, N.H.: Yankee Books, 1989.

### 106. Why did Moses have horns on his head?
Goodenough, Simon. *1500 Fascinating Facts.* London: Treasure Press, 1987.

Louis, David. *2201 Fascinating Facts.* New York: Crown Publishing, 1983.

Smith, Douglas B. *More Ever Wonder Why?* New York: Ballantine Books, 1994.

### 107. What American pastime started with a garage door and a projector?
Harris, Harry. *Good Old-Fashioned Yankee Ingenuity.* Chelsea, Mich.: Scarborough House, 1990.

King, Norman. *The Almanac of Fascinating Beginnings.* New York: Carol Publishing, 1994.

Tuleja, Tad. *Curious Customs.* New York: Stonesong Press, 1987.

### 108. How did the term *hangnail* happen?

Burnam, Tom. *The Dictionary of Misinformation.* New York: Ballantine Books, 1975.

Morris, William, and Mary Morris. *Morris Dictionary of Word and Phrase Origins.* 2d ed. New York: HarperCollins, 1988.

### 109. How did a captive audience escape from the singing emperor?

Asimov, Isaac. *Would You Believe?* New York: Grosset and Dunlap, 1982.

Tuleja, Tad. *The New York Public Library Book of Popular Americana.* New York: Macmillan, 1994.

### 110. Where would you find a nest egg?

Morris, William, and Mary Morris. *Morris Dictionary of Word and Phrase Origins.* 2d ed. New York: HarperCollins, 1988.

### 111. When was *Heidi* the most unpopular movie on television?

Goldberg, M. Hirsh. *The Blunder Book.* New York: William Morrow and Co., 1984.

### 112. What's so bad about good news?

Wallace, Irving, Amy Wallace, and David Wallechinsky. *Significa.* New York: E. P. Dutton, Inc., 1983.

### 113. How do the famous Nielson ratings work?

Sutton, Caroline. *How Do They Do That?* New York: Quill, 1982.

Sutton, Caroline, and Kevin Markey. *More How Do They Do That?* New York: William Morrow and Co., 1993.

### 114. Why don't doctors wear white like nurses?

Feldman, David. *Why Do Clocks Run Clockwise? and Other Imponderables.* New York: Harper and Row, 1987.

### 115. What was the job of the "official uncorker of bottles"?

Alway, Carol, et al. *Amazing Stories, Strange Facts.* New York: Reader's Digest Association, 1976.

### 116. What do checkers and cookies have in common?

Varasdi, J. Allen. *Myth Information.* New York: Ballantine Books, 1989.

### 117. Why is the Oscar named after a farmer?

Harris, Harry. *Good Old-Fashioned Yankee Ingenuity.* Chelsea, Mich.: Scarborough House, 1990.

Louis, David. *2201 Fascinating Facts.* New York: Crown Publishing, 1983.

Perko, Marko. *Did You Know That . . . ?* New York: Berkley Books, 1994.

*Ripley's Believe It or Not! Mind Teasers Far and Wide.* Mankato, Minn.: Capstone Press, 1991.

Tuleja, Tad. *The New York Public Library Book of Popular Americana.* New York: Macmillan, 1994.

### 118. How could someone lose a three-mile-long painting?

Felton, Bruce, and Mark Fowler. *Felton and Fowler's Best, Worst, and Most Unusual.* New York: Thomas Y. Crowell, 1975.

Fullerton, Timothy T. *Triviata: A Compendium of Useless Information.* New York: Hart Publishing, 1975.

Louis, David. *2201 Fascinating Facts.* New York: Crown Publishing, 1983.

Manchester, Richard B. *Incredible Facts.* New York: Galahad Books, 1985.

Morris, Scot. *The Emperor Who Ate the Bible and More Strange Facts and Useless Information.* New York: Doubleday, 1991.

Perko, Marko. *Did You Know That . . . ?* New York: Berkley Books, 1994.

Wallace, Irving, Amy Wallace, and David Wallechinsky. *Significa.* New York: E. P. Dutton, Inc., 1983.

### 119. Why wasn't the perfect book perfect?

Goldberg, M. Hirsh. *The Blunder Book.* New York: William Morrow and Co., 1984.

### 120. How are "scratch 'n' sniff" products made?

Hawkes, Nigel, et al. *How in the World?* New York: Reader's Digest Association, 1990.

### 121. What were cats once accused of causing?

Buchman, Dian Dincin, and Seli Groves. *What If? Fifty Discoveries That Changed the World.* New York: Scholastic, Inc., 1988.

Lee, Stan. *Stan Lee Presents the Best of the Worst.* New York: Harper and Row, 1979.

Lurie, Susan, ed. *The Big Book of Amazing Knowledge.* New York: Claymore, Inc., 1987.

*Simon and Schuster Color Illustrated Book of Questions and Answers.* New York: Simon and Schuster, 1986.

Urton, Andrea. *Now Entering Weirdsville!* Los Angeles: Lowell House, 1992.

Varasdi, J. Allen. *Myth Information.* New York: Ballantine Books, 1989.

### 122. Why do people have problems with plurals?

Burnam, Tom. *The Dictionary of Misinformation.* New York: Thomas Y. Crowell, 1975.

### 123. Why did the barber need a pole?

Flexner, Stuart Berg. *Listening to America.* New York: Simon and Schuster, 1982.

McCutcheon, Marc. *The Writer's Guide to Everyday Life in the 1800s.* Cincinnati, Ohio: Writer's Digest Books, 1993.

McLoughlin, E. V., ed. *The Book of Knowledge.* Vol. 13. New York: The Grolier Society, 1947.

Smith, Douglas B. *Ever Wonder Why?* New York: Ballantine Books, 1991.

Tuleja, Tad. *Curious Customs.* New York: Stonesong Press, 1987.

Vogel, Malvina G., ed. *The Big Book of Amazing Facts.* New York: Playmore, Inc., 1980.

### 124. Why are the sides of a boat called port and starboard?

*Charlie Brown's 'Cyclopedia.* Vol. 5. New York: Random House, 1980.

Claiborne, Robert. *Loose Cannons and Red Herrings.* New York: W. W. Norton and Co., 1988.

Funk, Charles Earle, and Charles Earle Funk Jr. *Horsefeathers and Other Curious Words.* New York: Harper and Row, 1958.

Parker, Steve. *How Things Are Made.* New York: Random House, 1993.

Smith, Douglas B. *Ever Wonder Why?* New York: Ballantine Books, 1991.

### 125. Which city was named by the toss of a coin?

Felton, Bruce. *One of a Kind.* New York: William Morrow and Co., 1992.

### 126. How is Thomas Jefferson connected to the potato chip?

Campbell, Hannah. *Why Did They Name It . . . ?* New York: Fleet Publishing, 1964.

Caney, Steven. *Steven Caney's Kids' America.* New York: Workman Publishing, 1978.

Choron, Sandra. *The Big Book of Kids' Lists.* New York: World Almanac Publications, 1985.

Felder, Deborah G. *The Kids' World Almanac of History.* New York: Pharos Books, 1991.

Flexner, Stuart Berg. *Listening to America.* New York: Simon and Schuster, 1982.

Gray, Ralph, ed. *Small Inventions That Make a Big Difference.* National Geographic Society, 1984.

Harris, Harry. *Good Old-Fashioned Yankee Ingenuity.* Chelsea, Mich.: Scarborough House, 1990.

Jones, Charlotte Foltz. *Mistakes That Worked.* New York: Doubleday, 1991.

King, Norman. *The Almanac of Fascinating Beginnings*. New York: Carol Publishing, 1994.

McLoone, Margo, and Alice Siegel. *The Kids' World Almanac of Records and Facts*. New York: World Almanac Publications, 1985.

Panati, Charles. *Panati's Extraordinary Origins of Everyday Things*. New York: Harper and Row, 1987.

Sutton, Caroline. *How Did They Do That?* New York: William Morrow and Co., 1984.

Taylor, Barbara. *Weekly Reader Presents Be an Inventor*. Orlando, Fla.: Harcourt, Brace, Jovanovich, 1987.

Tuleja, Tad. *Curious Customs*. New York: Stonesong Press, 1987.

**127. Why are detectives called private eyes?**

Flexner, Stuart Berg. *Listening to America*. New York: Simon and Schuster, 1982.

Sperling, Susan Kelz. *Tenderfeet and Ladyfingers*. New York: The Penguin Group, 1981.

Wallechinsky, David, and Irving Wallace. *The People's Almanac Presents the Book of Lists 2*. New York: Bantam Books, 1978.

**128. Who was Charles Boycott?**

Flexner, Stuart Berg. *Listening to America*. New York: Simon and Schuster, 1982.

Rovin, Jeff. *The Unbelievable Truth!* New York: The Penguin Group, 1994.

Smith, Douglas B. *More Ever Wonder Why?* New York: Ballantine Books, 1994.

Wallechinsky, David, and Irving Wallace. *The People's Almanac*. New York: Doubleday, 1975.

**129. What kind of puzzle took five years to solve?**

May, John. *Curious Facts*. New York: Holt, Rhinehart, and Winston, 1980.

**130. What is the dollar bill saying with symbols?**

Baecher, Charlotte, ed. "Money Talks." *Zillions*. January 1996.

Smith, Douglas B. *More Ever Wonder Why?* New York: Ballantine Books, 1994.

**131. How did an ocean liner get the wrong name?**

Harvey, Edmund, ed. *Reader's Digest Book of Facts*. New York: Reader's Digest Association, 1987.

**132. How did the question mark get its strange shape?**

Meyers, James. *Amazing Facts*. New York: Playmore, Inc., 1986.

Smith, Douglas B. *Ever Wonder Why?* New York: Ballantine Books, 1991.

**133. Why did the rainmaker lose his job?**

Alway, Carol, et al. *Strange Stories, Amazing Facts*. New York: Reader's Digest Association, 1976.

Felton, Bruce, and Mark Fowler. *Felton and Fowler's More Best, Worst, and Most Unusual*. New York: Fawcett Crest, 1976.

*Reader's Digest Facts and Fallacies*. New York: Reader's Digest Association, 1988.

Vogel, Malvina G., ed. *The Big Book of Amazing Facts*. New York: Playmore, Inc., 1980.

**134. What legacy did Henrietta Lacks leave?**

*Reader's Digest Facts and Fallacies*. New York: Reader's Digest Association, 1988.

**135. Which was worse—a snowstorm or a private meeting with the president?**

Lee, Stan. *Stan Lee Presents the Best of the Worst*. New York: Harper and Row, 1979.

**136. How was a wedding ring reclaimed after it was lost at sea?**

Alway, Carol, et al. *Strange Stories, Amazing Facts*. New York: Reader's Digest Association, 1976.

**137. Where does the asphalt go from a pothole?**

Feldman, David. *Why Do Clocks Run Clockwise? and Other Imponderables*. New York: Harper and Row, 1987.

Rovin, Jeff. *The Unbelievable Truth!* New York: The Penguin Group, 1994.

Smith, Douglas B. *Ever Wonder Why?* New York: Ballantine Books, 1991.

Williams, Brian, and Brenda Williams. *The Random House Book of 1001 Wonders of Science*. New York: Random House, 1990.

**138. Why was a bank alarmed about a withdrawal?**

Sobol, Donald J. *Encyclopedia Brown's Book of Wacky Crimes*. New York: E. P. Dutton, Inc., 1982.

**139. How do rocks travel in Death Valley?**

*Reader's Digest Facts and Fallacies*. New York: Reader's Digest Association, 1988.

Robbins, Pat, ed. *Why in the World?* Washington, D.C.: National Geographic Society, 1985.

**140. How did a fire alarm improve baking bread?**

Campbell, Hannah. *Why Did They Name It . . . ?* New York: Fleet Publishing, 1964.

Jones, Charlotte Foltz. *Mistakes That Worked.* New York: Doubleday, 1991.

**141. How do seeds always know to send their roots downward?**

Goldwyn, Martin M. *How a Fly Walks Upside Down . . . and Other Curious Facts.* New York: Carol Publishing, 1989.

Robbins, Pat, ed. *Why in the World?* Washington, D.C.: National Geographic Society, 1985.

Vogel, Malvina G., ed. *The Big Book of Amazing Facts.* New York: Playmore, Inc., 1980.

**142. How did restaurants start from the French Revolution?**

Flexner, Stuart Berg. *Listening to America.* New York: Simon and Schuster, 1982.

Meyers, James. *Eggplants, Elevators, Etc.: An Uncommon History of Common Things.* New York: Hart Publishing, 1978.

**143. Why is the ocean so salty?**

Feldman, David. *Do Penguins Have Knees?* HarperCollins, 1991.

Fullerton, Timothy T. *Triviata: A Compendium of Useless Information.* New York: Hart Publishing, 1975.

Goldwyn, Martin M. *How a Fly Walks Upside Down . . . and Other Curious Facts.* New York: Carol Publishing, 1979.

*Johnny Wonder Question and Answer Book.* New York: Playmore, Inc., 1984.

Louis, David. *2201 Fascinating Facts.* New York: Crown Publishing, 1983.

Rosenbloom, Joseph. *Polar Bears Like It Hot.* New York: Sterling Publishing, 1980.

*Simon and Schuster Color Illustrated Book of Questions and Answers.* New York: Simon and Schuster, 1986.

Smith, Douglas B. *Ever Wonder Why?* New York: Ballantine Books, 1991.

Vogel, Malvina G., ed. *The Big Book of Amazing Facts.* New York: Playmore, Inc., 1980.

Williams, Brian, and Brenda Williams. *The Random House Book of 1001 Wonders of Science.* New York: Random House, 1990.

**144. What is the history of the sandwich?**

Alway, Carol, et al. *Strange Stories, Amazing Facts.* New York: Reader's Digest Association, 1976.

Buchman, Dian Dincin, and Seli Groves. *What If? Fifty Discoveries That Changed the World.* New York: Scholastic, Inc., 1988.

Epstein, Sam, and Beryl Epstein. *What's behind the Word?* New York: Scholastic, Inc., 1964.

Felder, Deborah G. *The Kids' World Almanac of History.* New York: Pharos Books, 1991.

Flexner, Stuart Berg. *Listening to America.* New York: Simon and Schuster, 1982.

Goodenough, Simon. *1500 Fascinating Facts.* London: Treasure Press, 1987.

Jones, Charlotte Foltz. *Mistakes That Worked.* New York: Doubleday, 1991.

Limburg, Peter R. *Stories behind Words.* New York: H. W. Wilson, 1986.

McLoone, Margo, and Alice Siegel. *The Kids' World Almanac of Records and Facts.* New York: World Almanac Publications, 1986.

Panati, Charles. *Panati's Extraordinary Origins of Everyday Things.* New York: Harper and Row, 1987.

Perko, Marko. *Did You Know That . . . ?* New York: Berkley Books, 1994.

Rovin, Jeff. *The Unbelievable Truth!* New York: The Penguin Group, 1994.

Vogel, Malvina G., ed. *The Big Book of Amazing Facts.* New York: Playmore, Inc., 1980.

## 145. Why is it impossible to buy fresh sardines?

Burnam, Tom. *The Dictionary of Misinformation.* New York: Ballantine Books, 1975.

Feldman, David. *Imponderables.* New York: William Morrow and Co., 1986.

Fullerton, Timothy T. *Triviata: A Compendium of Useless Information.* New York: Hart Publishing, 1975.

Varasdi, J. Allen. *Myth Information.* New York: Ballantine Books, 1989.

## 146. How do you return the favor of a rescue?

Wulffson, Don L. *Amazing True Stories.* New York: Scholastic, Inc., 1991.

## 147. Why don't birds seem frightened by scarecrows?

Vogel, Malvina G., ed. *The Big Book of Amazing Facts.* New York: Playmore, Inc., 1980.

## 148. Why was telling time tricky on trains?

Flexner, Stuart Berg. *Listening to America.* New York: Simon and Schuster, 1982.

Harris, Harry. *Good Old-Fashioned Yankee Ingenuity.* Chelsea, Mich.: Scarborough House, 1990.

Vogel, Malvina G., ed. *The Big Book of Amazing Facts.* New York: Playmore, Inc., 1980.

Wallace, Irving, Amy Wallace, and David Wallechinsky. *Significa*. New York: E. P. Dutton, Inc., 1983.

**149. When were dirty tennis shoes helpful?**
Jones, Charlotte Foltz. *Mistakes That Worked*. New York: Doubleday, 1991.

**150. What's the best way to clean?**
Florman, Monte. *1,001 Helpful Tips, Facts and Hints from Consumer Reports*. Mount Vernon, N.Y.: Consumer's Union of U.S., Inc., 1989.

**151. How was the peace sign developed?**
Rovin, Jeff. *The Unbelievable Truth!* New York: The Penguin Group, 1994.
Smith, Douglas B. *More Ever Wonder Why?* New York: Ballantine Books, 1994.
Vogel, Malvina G., ed. *The Big Book of Amazing Facts*. New York: Playmore, Inc., 1980.

**152. What were the shortest letters ever written?**
Vogel, Malvina G., ed. *The Big Book of Amazing Facts*. New York: Playmore, Inc., 1980.
Sobol, Donald J. *Encyclopedia Brown's Second Record Book of Weird and Wonderful Facts*. New York: Delacorte Press, 1981.

**153. What does it mean to give someone the cold shoulder?**
Alway, Carol, et al. *Strange Stories, Amazing Facts*. New York: Reader's Digest Association, 1976.
Flexner, Stuart Berg. *Listening to America*. New York: Simon and Schuster, 1982.
McLoone, Margo, and Alice Siegel. *The Second Kids' World Almanac of Records and Facts*. New York: World Almanac Publications, 1987.
Rovin, Jeff. *The Unbelievable Truth!* New York: The Penguin Group, 1994.
Smith, Douglas B. *Ever Wonder Why?* New York: Ballantine Books, 1991.
Sperling, Susan Kelz. *Tenderfeet and Ladyfingers*. New York: The Penguin Group, 1981.

**154. How did sideburns get their name?**
Burnam, Tom. *The Dictionary of Misinformation*. New York: Ballantine Books, 1975.
Flexner, Stuart Berg. *Listening to America*. New York: Simon and Schuster, 1982.
Limburg, Peter R. *Stories behind Words*. New York: H. W. Wilson, 1986.
Morris, William, and Mary Morris. *Morris Dictionary of Word and Phrase Origins*. 2d ed. New York: Harper and Row, 1988.

Smith, Douglas B. *More Ever Wonder Why?* New York: Ballantine Books, 1994.

**155. How did a broken church organ inspire the creation of a carol?**
Louis, David. *2201 Fascinating Facts.* New York: Crown Publishing, 1983.
Wallace, Irving, Amy Wallace, and David Wallechinsky. *Significa.* New York: E. P. Dutton, Inc., 1983.

**156. Who was Simon in the game Simon Says?**
Rovin, Jeff. *The Unbelievable Truth!* New York: The Penguin Group, 1994.
Smith, Douglas B. *More Ever Wonder Why?* New York: Ballantine Books, 1994.

**157. How did a dog help save a city?**
Alway, Carol, et al. *Strange Stories, Amazing Facts.* New York: Reader's Digest Association, 1976.
McLoughlin, E. V., ed. *The Book of Knowledge.* Vol. 15. New York: The Grolier Society, Inc., 1947.

**158. Why wasn't Miss National Smile Princess smiling?**
Pile, Stephen. *The Book of Heroic Failures.* London: Routledge and Kegan Paul, Ltd., 1979.

**159. How are Social Security numbers selected?**
Louis, David. *2201 Fascinating Facts.* New York: Crown Publishing, 1983.
Morris, Scot. *The Emperor Who Ate the Bible and More Strange Facts and Useless Information.* New York: Doubleday, 1991.

**160. Does sound always travel at the same speed?**
Goldwyn, Martin M. *How a Fly Walks Upside Down . . . and Other Curious Facts.* New York: Carol Publishing, 1989.
Perko, Marko. *Did You Know That . . . ?* New York: Berkley Books, 1994.
Varasdi, J. Allen. *Myth Information.* New York: Ballantine Books, 1989.

**161. Does spinach really make you strong?**
Harvey, Edmund, ed. *Reader's Digest Book of Facts.* New York: Reader's Digest Association, 1987.
McKenzie, E. C. *Salted Peanuts: 1800 Little Known Facts.* Grand Rapids, Mich.: Baker Book House, 1972.
*Reader's Digest Facts and Fallacies.* New York: Reader's Digest Association, 1988.
Rowan, Dr. Peter. *Can You Get Warts from Touching Toads?* New York: Julian Messner, 1986.

Simon, Seymour. *Body Sense, Body Nonsense.* New York: J. B. Lippencott, 1981.

Smith, Douglas B. *More Ever Wonder Why?* New York: Ballantine Books, 1994.

Tuleja, Tad. *Fabulous Fallacies.* South Yarmouth, Mass.: John Curley and Associates, Inc., 1982.

### 162. How did stamp collecting start?
Vogel, Malvina G., ed. *The Big Book of Amazing Facts.* New York: Playmore, Inc., 1980.

### 163. What secrets are some statues saying?
Rovin, Jeff. *The Unbelievable Truth!* New York: The Penguin Group, 1994.

Smith, Douglas B. *More Ever Wonder Why?* New York: Ballantine Books, 1994.

### 164. Why does the man walk next to the curb when escorting a woman?
Smith, Douglas B. *More Ever Wonder Why?* New York: Ballantine Books, 1994.

Tuleja, Tad. *Curious Customs.* New York: Stonesong Press, 1987.

Vogel, Malvina G., ed. *The Big Book of Amazing Facts.* New York: Playmore, Inc., 1980.

### 165. Can you name one number that never changes?
Harvey, Edmund, ed. *Reader's Digest Book of Facts.* New York: Reader's Digest Association, 1987.

### 166. Why would anyone ask the enemy for advice during a war?
Wallace, Irving, Amy Wallace, and David Wallechinsky. *Significa.* New York: E. P. Dutton, Inc., 1983.

### 167. What's the story behind the Taj Mahal?
Hicks, Donna E. *The Most Fascinating Places on Earth.* New York: Sterling Publishing, 1993.

Lurie, Susan, ed. *A Treasury of Amazing Knowledge.* New York: Playmore, Inc., 1988.

### 168. How was masking tape invented?
Alway, Carol, et al. *Strange Stories, Amazing Facts.* New York: Reader's Digest Association, 1976.

Campbell, Hannah. *Why Did They Name It . . . ?* New York: Fleet Publishing, 1964.

Caney, Steven. *Steven Caney's Invention Book.* New York: Workman Publishing, 1985.

Giscard d'Estaing, Valerie-Anne. *Inventions.* New York: World Almanac Publications, 1985.

Harris, Harry. *Good Old-Fashioned Yankee Ingenuity.* Chelsea, Mich.: Scarborough House, 1990.

Landau, Irwin, ed. *I'll Buy That.* New York: Consumer's Union, 1986.

Lurie, Susan, ed. *The Treasury of Amazing Knowledge.* New York: Playmore, Inc., 1988.

Rovin, Jeff. *The Unbelievable Truth!* New York: The Penguin Group, 1994.

Smith, Douglas B. *More Ever Wonder Why?* New York: Ballantine Books, 1994.

Sutton, Caroline. *How Did They Do That?* New York: William Morrow and Co., 1984.

### 169. What was brewing over the tea bag?

Buchman, Dian Dincin, and Seli Groves. *What If? Fifty Discoveries That Changed the World.* New York: Scholastic, Inc., 1988.

Flexner, Stuart Berg. *Listening to America.* New York: Simon and Schuster, 1982.

Jones, Charlotte Foltz. *Mistakes That Worked.* New York: Doubleday, 1991.

Smith, Douglas B. *More Ever Wonder Why?* New York: Ballantine Books, 1994.

### 170. How does thunder get stolen?

Meyers, James. *Amazing Facts.* New York: Playmore, Inc., 1986.

Rovin, Jeff. *The Unbelievable Truth!* New York: The Penguin Group, 1994.

Smith, Douglas B. *Ever Wonder Why?* New York: Ballantine Books, 1991.

Vanoni, Marvin. *Great Expressions.* New York: William Morrow and Co., 1989.

### 171. Why do men wear neckties?

Giscard d'Estaing, Valerie-Anne. *Inventions.* New York: World Almanac Publications, 1985.

Harris, Harry. *Good Old-Fashioned Yankee Ingenuity.* Chelsea, Mich.: Scarborough House, 1990.

Lurie, Susan, ed. *A Treasury of Amazing Knowledge.* New York: Playmore, Inc., 1988.

Meyers, James. *Amazing Facts.* New York: Playmore, Inc., 1986.

Panati, Charles. *Panati's Extraordinary Origins of Everyday Things.* New York: Harper and Row, 1987.

Rovin, Jeff. *The Unbelievable Truth!* New York: The Penguin Group, 1994.

Smith, Douglas B. *Ever Wonder Why?* New York: Ballantine Books, 1991.

Sutton, Caroline. *How Did They Do That?* New York: William Morrow and Co., 1984.

### 172. Why were wedding rings collected at a tollbooth?

Wallace, Irving, Amy Wallace, and David Wallechinsky. *Significa*. New York: E. P. Dutton, Inc., 1983.

Wulffson, Don L. *Amazing True Stories*. New York: Scholastic, Inc., 1991.

### 173. Why was a tomato taken to trial?

Perko, Marko. *Did You Know That . . . ?* New York: Berkley Books, 1994.

Vogel, Malvina G., ed. *The Big Book of Amazing Facts*. New York: Playmore, Inc., 1980.

Wallace, Irving, Amy Wallace, and David Wallechinsky. *Significa*. New York: E. P. Dutton, Inc., 1983.

### 174. Why does the Leaning Tower of Pisa lean?

Goldberg, M. Hirsh. *The Blunder Book*. New York: William Morrow and Co., 1984.

Goodenough, Simon. *1500 Fascinating Facts*. London: Treasure Press, 1987.

Jones, Charlotte Foltz. *Mistakes That Worked*. New York: Doubleday, 1991.

Pringle, Laurence. *"The Earth Is Flat" and Other Great Mistakes*. New York: William Morrow and Co., 1983.

*Reader's Digest Facts and Fallacies*. New York: Reader's Digest Association, Inc., 1988.

Smith, Douglas B. *More Ever Wonder Why?* New York: Ballantine Books, 1994.

Tuleja, Ted. *Fabulous Fallacies*. South Yarmouth, Mass.: John Curley and Associates, Inc., 1982.

Vogel, Malvina G., ed. *The Big Book of Amazing Facts*. New York: Playmore, Inc., 1980.

Wallace, Irving, Amy Wallace, and David Wallechinsky. *Significa*. New York: E. P. Dutton, Inc., 1983.

### 175. Why do police cars use blue lights?

Smith, Douglas B. *Ever Wonder Why?* New York: Ballantine Books, 1991.

### 176. What historical stories do nursery rhymes tell?

Alway, Carol, et. al. *Strange Stories, Amazing Facts*. New York: Reader's Digest Association, 1976.

Goodenough, Simon. *1500 Fascinating Facts*. London: Treasure Press, 1987.

Louis, David. *2201 Fascinating Facts*. New York: Crown Publishing, 1983.

Opie, Iona, and Peter Opie, eds. *The Oxford Nursery Rhyme Book*. London: Oxford University Press, 1955.

### 177. Why did the president's son take a book to the inauguration?

Louis, David. *2201 Fascinating Facts*. New York: Crown Publishing, 1983.

Perko, Marko. *Did You Know That . . . ?* New York: Berkley Books, 1994.

Seuling, Barbara. *The Last Cow on the White House Lawn and Other Little Known Facts about the President*. New York: Doubleday, 1978.

Stevenson, Robert Louis. *Treasure Island*. New York: Henry Holt and Co., 1993.

### 178. Who wouldn't accept a check from the treasury secretary?

Morris, Scot. *The Emperor Who Ate the Bible and More Strange Facts and Useless Information*. New York: Doubleday, 1991.

### 179. How did the washing machine change wash day?

Aylward, Jim. *Your Burro Is No Jackass! And Over 100 Other Things No One Ever Told You*. New York: Holt, Rinehart, and Winston, 1981.

Ewing, Elizabeth. *Everyday Dress*. New York: Chelsea House Publishers, 1984.

Felder, Deborah G. *The Kids' World Almanac of History*. New York: Pharos Books, 1991.

Giscard d'Estaing, Valerie-Anne. *Inventions*. New York: World Almanac Publications, 1985.

Harris, Harry. *Good Old-Fashioned Yankee Ingenuity*. Chelsea, Mich.: Scarborough House, 1990.

Landau, Irwin, ed. *I'll Buy That*. New York: Consumers Union, 1986.

### 180. Who wanted the same birthday present every year?

Harvey, Edmund, ed. *Reader's Digest Book of Facts*. New York: Reader's Digest Association, 1987.

### 181. Does your kitchen contain this invention?

Aaseng, Nathan. *Better Mousetraps*. Minneapolis: Lerner Publications, 1990.

King, Norman. *The Almanac of Fascinating Beginnings*. New York: Carol Publishing, 1994.

Giscard d'Estaing, Valerie-Anne. *Inventions*. New York: World Almanac Publications, 1985.

Harris, Harry. *Good Old-Fashioned Yankee Ingenuity.* Chelsea, Mich.: Scarborough House, 1990.

Publishers of *Yankee Magazine. The Inventive Yankee.* Dublin, N.H.: Yankee Books, 1989.

Tuleja, Tad. *Curious Customs.* New York: Stonesong Press, 1987.

### 182. Who was "Typhoid Mary"?

Burnam, Tom. *The Dictionary of Misinformation.* New York: Ballantine Books, 1975.

Felton, Bruce, and Mark Fowler. *Felton and Fowler's More Best, Worst, and Most Unusual.* New York: Fawcett Crest, 1976.

Fullerton, Timothy T. *Triviata: A Compendium of Useless Information.* New York: Hart Publishing, 1975.

Smith, Richard, and Edward Decter. *Oops! The Complete Book of Bloopers.* New York: The Rutledge Press, 1981.

Varasdi, J. Allen. *Myth Information.* New York: Ballantine Books, 1989.

Wallechinsky, David, Irving Wallace, and Amy Wallace. *The Book of Lists.* New York: Bantam Books, 1978.

### 183. Why are veins blue when blood is red?

Tuleja, Tad. *Fabulous Fallacies.* South Yarmouth, Mass.: John Curley and Associates, Inc., 1982.

Varasdi, J. Allen. *Myth Information.* New York: Ballantine Books, 1989.

Whitfield, Dr. Philip, and Dr. Ruth Whitfield. *Why Do Our Bodies Stop Growing? Questions about the Human Anatomy Answered by the Natural History Museum.* New York: Viking, 1988.

### 184. Why is the bottom button of a man's vest left undone?

Tuleja, Tad. *Curious Customs.* New York: Crown Publishing, 1987.

### 185. When did a solution become a growing problem?

Goldberg, M. Hirsh. *The Blunder Book.* New York: William Morrow and Co., 1984.

Pringle, Laurence. *"The Earth Is Flat" and Other Great Mistakes.* New York: William Morrow and Co., 1983.

### 186. How do you interpret the results of a vision test?

Goldwyn, Martin M. *How a Fly Walks Upside Down . . . and Other Curious Facts.* New York: Carol Publishing, 1979.

Rovin, Jeff. *The Unbelievable Truth!* New York: The Penguin Group, 1994.

Seuling, Barbara. *You Can't Sneeze with Your Eyes Open.* New York: E. P. Dutton, Inc., 1986.

**187. What was the best investment that was ever made on Wall Street?**

Burnam, Tom. *The Dictionary of Misinformation.* New York: Ballantine Books, 1975.

Flexner, Stuart Berg. *Listening to America.* New York: Simon and Schuster, 1982.

Meyers, James. *Jumbo Amazing Question and Answer Book.* New York: Playmore, Inc., 1990.

Perko, Marko. *Did You Know That . . . ?* New York: Berkley Books, 1994.

Vanoni, Marvin. *Great Expressions.* New York: William Morrow and Co., 1989.

**188. Why would a family throw glass balls at a fire?**

Giscard d'Estaing, Valerie-Anne. *Inventions.* New York: World Almanac Publications, 1985.

Leokum, Arkady. *The Curious Book.* New York: Sterling Publishing, 1976.

Louis, David. *2201 Fascinating Facts.* New York: Crown Publishing, 1983.

Robertson, Patrick. *The Book of Firsts.* New York: Bramhall House, 1974.

Vogel, Malvina G., ed. *The Big Book of Amazing Facts.* New York: Playmore, Inc., 1980.

Williams, Brenda, and Brian Williams. *The Random House Book of 1001 Wonders of Science.* New York: Random House, 1990.

**189. Why was someone ironing dollar bills?**

Wallace, Irving, Amy Wallace, and David Wallechinsky. *Significa.* New York: E. P. Dutton, Inc., 1983.

**190. Who tried to control the ocean?**

Harvey, Edmund, ed. *Reader's Digest Book of Facts.* New York: Reader's Digest Association, 1987.

**191. Where goes the bride?**

Burnam, Tom. *The Dictionary of Misinformation.* New York: Ballantine Books, 1975.

Varasdi, J. Allen. *Myth Information.* New York: Ballantine Books, 1989.

**192. Why was a statue dedicated to a bug?**

Felton, Bruce. *One of a Kind.* New York: William Morrow and Co., 1992.

**193. Why is the windchill colder than the air temperature?**

Burnam, Tom. *More Misinformation.* New York: Ballantine Books, 1980.

Lurie, Susan, ed. *The Big Book of Amazing Knowledge.* New York: Playmore, Inc., 1987.

**194. Why were windshield wipers invented?**
Buchman, Dian Dincin, and Seli Groves. *What If? Fifty Discoveries That Changed the World.* New York: Scholastic, Inc., 1988.

**195. Why do we call them "wisdom teeth"?**
Feldman, David. *Why Do Clocks Run Clockwise? and Other Imponderables.* New York: Harper and Row, 1987.
Meyers, James. *Amazing Facts.* New York: Playmore, Inc., 1986.

**196. How did a lost cabby help save a life?**
Morris, Scot. *The Emperor Who Ate the Bible and More Strange Facts and Useless Information.* New York: Doubleday, 1991.

**197. What were sheep doing at the White House?**
Louis, David. *2201 Fascinating Facts.* New York: Crown Publishing, 1983.
McKenzie, E. C. *Salted Peanuts: 1800 Little Known Facts.* Grand Rapids, Mich.: Baker Book House, 1972.
Smith, Douglas B. *More Ever Wonder Why?* New York: Ballantine Books, 1994.
Wallace, Irving, Amy Wallace, and David Wallechinsky. *Significa.* New York: E. P. Dutton, Inc., 1983.

**198. What does the *X* in *Xmas* stand for?**
Burnam, Tom. *The Dictionary of Misinformation.* New York: Ballantine Books, 1975.
Feldman, David. *Why Do Clocks Run Clockwise? and Other Imponderables.* New York: Harper and Row, 1987.
Louis, David. *2201 Fascinating Facts.* New York: Crown Publishing, 1983.
Perko, Marko. *Did You Know That . . . ?* New York: Berkley Books, 1994.
Rovin, Jeff. *The Unbelievable Truth.* New York: The Penguin Group, 1994.
Smith, Douglas B. *More Ever Wonder Why?* New York: Ballantine Books, 1994.
Tuleja, Tad. *Curious Customs.* New York: Stonesong Press, 1987.

**199. Why are cowards considered yellow?**
Smith, Douglas B. *Ever Wonder Why?* New York: Ballantine Books, 1991.

**200. What were deeds doing in cereal boxes?**
Wallace, Irving, Amy Wallace, and David Wallechinsky. *Significa.* New York: E. P. Dutton, Inc., 1983.